VICTORIA BLAKE

# Mrs Maybrick

the national archives

First published in 2008 by
The National Archives
Kew, Richmond
Surrey, TW9 4DU, UK
www.nationalarchives.gov.uk

The National Archives
brings together the Public Record Office,
Historical Manuscripts Commission,
Office of Public Sector Information
and Her Majesty's Stationery Office.

A catalogue card for this book is available from the British Library.

ISBN 978 1 905615 18 6

Cover illustrations: portraits of Florence Maybrick (registered
for copyright 14 August 1889; COPY 1 397/247) and her husband
James Maybrick (circa 1880; Getty Images)
Jacket design and page typesetting by Goldust Design
Page design and plate section typesetting by Ken Wilson | point 918
Picture research by Gwen Campbell
Printed in Germany by
Bercker Graphischer Betrieb GmbH & Co

# Contents

————

I am writing to you to give me every assistance in your power in my present fearful trouble. I am in custody without any of my family with me and without money. I have called to my solicitor in New York to come here at once. In the meantime send some money for my present needs. The truth is known about my visit to London. Your last letter is in the hands of the police. Appearances may be against me, but before God I swear I am innocent. (HO 144/1638/A50678)

Letter from Florence Maybrick to Alfred Brierley

# Cause Célèbre

During the sweltering first week of August 1889 a young American named Florence Maybrick was tried in Liverpool for the murder of her English husband. It was a trial that gripped the imagination of Victorian society and created a huge furore on both sides of the Atlantic. The telegraph wires hummed with each day's sensational events. The story, played out before the eyes of a multitude of witnesses, including backbiting servants and in-laws, doctors and family friends, was a particularly juicy one involving sex, drugs and arsenic poisoning. At the heart of it was Mrs Maybrick herself (see plate 9), a pretty young widow, a foreigner with a colourful background, who had married a respected member of Liverpool's commercial elite.

By the time the drama was over Florence would be the subject of a three-act play called *The Poisoner* at Sadler's Wells Theatre and of innumerable books, including *Strong Poison* (1930) by Dorothy L. Sayers. A waxwork figure of her dressed in widow's weeds, holding a handkerchief soaked in arsenic, would be on display in Madame Tussaud's, and in 1922 she would even garner a mention from Molly Bloom as a 'downright villain' in James Joyce's *Ulysses*.

In addition Queen Victoria and her ministers in five governments would be drawn into the case, as would three presidents of the United States and their secretaries of state. Florence would be the subject of debate in the House of Commons and on the floor of Congress. The opinions of the legal and medical professions would be split down the middle and, as Trevor Christie writes in his excellent book *Etched in Arsenic*, the press with 'pens dipped in vitriol' would have discussed the case from every possible angle.

The case led to two important changes in the law. The first was the Criminal Evidence Act of 1898, which for the first time allowed a person accused of murder to give evidence on their own behalf. When Mrs Maybrick was put on trial this was not permitted. Unusually the judge allowed her to make a statement from the dock, but she was not allowed to receive legal advice, or to call witnesses to corroborate her version of events. The statement she gave was generally viewed as being disastrous for her.

The second change was the creation of a criminal Court of Appeal in 1907. The conduct of the Maybrick trial by Judge Stephen had given rise to concerns about his mental fitness. One thing that particularly struck local journalists was that he appeared at one point in his summing up not to know what the Grand National was. To the inhabitants of Liverpool this was bizarre indeed. He was a well-respected judge, but had suffered from a stroke four years earlier and his mind was clearly befuddled. One of Florence's American supporters, Gail Hamilton, was later to describe him colourfully in an article 'In Defence of Mrs Maybrick', published in the New York *World* in September 1891, as being in the grip of 'a menacing mental calamity'. Six years after his death in August 1900, an editorial in the *Liverpool Daily Post* described him as the 'great, mad judge' in whom 'the light of reason was burning very low' during the trial (quoted from Anne E. Graham and Carol Emmas, *The Last Victim*).

Apart from these important legal changes, the case is also interesting for what it demonstrates about Victorian attitudes to women. Essentially they were second-class citizens. Not until 1882 did the Married Women's Property Act give them the rights to own property in their own names and to keep their own earnings. On the one hand respectable Victorian women were highly idealized as 'the angel in the home' and were seen as innocent creatures in need of male protection. The other side of this idealization however was demonization. Women were also viewed as 'innately prone to corruption'. After all, it was Eve who had tempted Adam and produced man's fall from grace.

The sexual double standards of the era are neatly summed up in the provisions of the Divorce and Matrimonial Causes Act 1857, which was designed to enable moderately wealthy men to divorce their wives. Men could seek a divorce on the grounds of their wife's adultery alone, but women had to prove adultery plus incest, bigamy, cruelty or desertion.

Florence undoubtedly suffered from these double standards. Much was made before and during the trial of the fact that, six weeks before her husband's death, she had decided to embark on an affair with a man called Alfred Brierley. A letter that she wrote to her lover on 8 May 1889, three days before her husband died, was intercepted (see plate 10). It was read out in the Coroner's Court, two months before the trial began, in front of 40 reporters and caused a sensation when it was widely reproduced in the papers.

So when the trial began Mrs Maybrick had already been found guilty in the press, her affair being seen as a motive for killing her husband. In his summing up Judge Stephen placed a great deal of emphasis on her adultery and failed to remind the jury of something that had been only cursorily alluded to by the defence in the trial, namely that James Maybrick had a long-standing mistress. This woman, surprisingly, had not been called as a defence witness. But if Florence was, as the judge described her, 'a horrible woman' for her affair with Brierley, then surely her husband was a horrible man? Not according to the judge, nor to the mores of the time or the all male jury.

The Maybrick trial is also of interest because of the role played by the press. There had been a huge growth in the number and circulation of newspapers during the nineteenth century. In London the number of daily papers rose from eight in 1856 to 21 in 1900. The first provincial dailies appeared in 1855 in Birmingham, Manchester, Sheffield and Liverpool. By

1885, 47 English towns had daily papers. The *Daily Telegraph*, a penny daily which launched in 1855, had a circulation of 300,000 by 1888.

In 1814, the largest selling newspaper, *The Times*, had switched to a steam press which increased the number of impressions that could be produced per hour from 250 to 1,000. From the late 1860s web rotary presses, which could print directly on to continuous rolls or webs of paper, were introduced in Britain. And in the mid-nineteenth century the so called 'taxes on knowledge' were abolished—advertisement duties in 1853, newspaper stamp duty in 1855 and paper duties in 1861.

The result was that newspapers became cheaper and more readily available. This was the birth of what we would recognize today as the sleazy tabloid press. And much like today, the press had a voracious appetite for the shocking and the titillating, and in particular stories about the royal family, divorce cases, and of course murder trials.

The trial of Florence Maybrick was exactly the kind of case it thrived on. The papers were all over it from the first day of the coroner's inquest, and their tone was universally hostile to Florence. However, almost as soon as the trial had begun and Florence's famous defending counsel, Sir Charles Russell, QC, got his teeth into the prosecution witnesses, the papers started to change their minds as a rather different picture appeared. The medical evidence was less than clear-cut, some doctors saying that James Maybrick's death was caused by arsenic poisoning, others making a case for gastro-enteritis; for the first time it was revealed that not enough arsenic was found in the victim's body to kill him. Then there was the revelation that Maybrick had a mistress and was an habitual drug user. During the trial, public opinion underwent a complete volte-face, and the spectators who had been hissing at Florence at the start were soon spitting at the prosecution witnesses.

Perhaps the most intriguing aspect of the case is the enigma that is Mrs Maybrick. Was she guilty or not guilty? Did she or didn't she try to poison her husband? It is a secret she took with her to her grave. She proclaimed her innocence—but what guilty person doesn't?

## TRANSATLANTIC ROMANCE

Florence Chandler first met James Maybrick in the bar of a transatlantic liner, the SS *Baltic*, as it steamed out of New York harbour on the way to Liverpool. The year was 1880. She was 18 years old, a Southern belle born in Mobile, Alabama; he a 42-year-old Liverpudlian cotton merchant. Eight days later when they disembarked in England they were engaged to be married.

It is easy to see what James saw in Florence. She was five foot two, petite, pretty and vivacious, with violet-blue eyes. She spoke fluent French and German, and displayed the sophistication of a young woman who had spent a lot of her childhood in Europe and had been educated by private governesses. She counted among her ancestors the first Episcopal bishop of Illinois and Lincoln's Secretary of the Treasury and Chief Justice. Her father, a Mobile banker, had died in 1863 when she was a baby. Her mother, a flamboyant character, remarried; that husband also died, and she moved to Europe with her children and married a German cavalry officer, the Baron von Roques. The combination of faded American aristocracy and a touch of European Bohemianism must have made Florence's background an intriguing one.

Florence's attraction to James is perhaps more surprising. Pictures of him at the time show a classic Victorian gentleman, rather portly, with a broad somewhat bovine face, large eyes and a droopy moustache (see plate 7). But he, like Florence, was an experienced transatlantic traveller; his business required regular trips to his office in Norfolk, Virginia, one of the largest cotton ports in America. John Aunspaugh, an American colleague in the cotton trade, described him as 'one of the straightest, most upright and honourable men in a business transaction I have known' (Christie). Maybe Florence was attracted to his success and apparent stolid respectability; maybe she wanted to lead a more secure life than the one she had so far experienced, a life characterized by her mother's incessant travels, precarious love life and financial crises. Was she looking for a father figure? It's more likely that James seemed familiar to her because like her mother he was a reckless charmer and not quite what he appeared. While he exaggerated the success of his cotton business, the Baroness let slip that Florence would one day inherit vast amounts of land in the Southern states of America. She probably didn't say that the title to the lands was disputed and that a lot of it was swamp. Greed fuelled by lies influenced both James and the Baroness to think favourably of the potential match.

Whatever the nature of the attraction, Florence and James were married in July 1881 at St James's, Piccadilly. Her dress was made of ivory satin as was her husband's waistcoat, which was embroidered with silver threaded roses and lilies of the valley. In the society columns Florence was described—not altogether accurately, as she only brought with her a dowry of a few hundred dollars a year—as an 'American heiress'.

## WEDDED BLISS

For the first three years of their marriage Florence and James lived half the year in Liverpool and half the year in Norfolk, Virginia, but in 1884 they returned to Liverpool permanently. The city was at that time a busy, thriving port (see plate 1), which handled nearly a third of all Great Britain's imports and exports along with four-fifths of her trade with America. The River Mersey was known as the 'river of ten thousand masts'. Ten of the largest shipping lines, including Cunard and White Star, made their bases in Liverpool and operated weekly sailings to the United States. The docks attracted labourers from

Scotland, Ireland and Wales; some stayed and settled while others paid the four guineas cost of a steerage ticket and headed for the 'New World' offered by America. Liverpool was also the destination of over a quarter of a million bales of cotton yearly, and cotton was James's trade. As a writer at the time said: 'Trade was enthroned with cotton as Prime Minister.' It was also the home of sprawling slums and nearly five hundred brothels.

Four years after their return the Maybricks moved into Battlecrease House in Aigburth, a prosperous Liverpool suburb inhabited by the burgeoning mercantile class (see plate 3). By this time they had two children: James was born in March 1882 and Gladys in June 1886. The house (which they rented) had three storeys and 20 rooms, and required a substantial staff. Alice Yapp (appropriately named as it turned out) was the nanny, Mrs Humphreys, the cook; there were two housemaids, Mary Cadwallader and Elizabeth Brierley, known as Bessie (no relation to Alfred Brierley); and also Mr Grant, the gardener, and his wife, Alice.

A frequent visitor to the house was a Mrs Briggs (née Janion) who had at one time been engaged to James Maybrick. She had three sisters, including a Mrs Hughes and a Miss Gertrude Janion who also visited; until James's marriage the family had had high hopes that he might marry one of the two unmarried sisters. One wonders what they thought of his new bride. It wasn't even as if she came with a lot of money.

Michael Maybrick (see plate 6) felt similarly. Though the

youngest of James's brothers he was the most influential in family affairs, having made a huge financial and popular success from his career as a songwriter under the name Stephen Adams. He did not like the look of Florence or the Baroness, suspecting them both of being adventuresses. James's other brothers Edwin, a cotton broker like James, and Thomas, a shipping agent, were less vocal in their criticisms.

These early years seem to have been mainly happy. There were some problems over Florence's mother's perpetually precarious finances and her demands for money. The Baroness was quick to complain in a letter to her solicitor David Armstrong in 1885 that James 'does not prove a son to me' (quoted in Graham and Emmas), presumably meaning he was not willing to support her. And in April 1885 Florence's brother, Holbrook, who was studying medicine in France, died of tuberculosis.

Florence appears during this time to have been a devoted wife and mother. In 1886 young James caught scarlet fever, and while his father took baby Gladys to Wales Florence stayed behind for six weeks and nursed him back to health. She also had a busy social life which included dinner parties, teas, card parties, balls and visits to the races. She loved fine clothes, and once when James teased her about a hole in her stockings which opened as she walked down the street she burst into anguished sobs. John Aunspaugh, visiting from America, described Florence at a dinner party given for him as wearing a fawn silk evening gown trimmed with dark purple velvet and ecru Brussels lace.

According to his account she loved male admiration just as much as she loved her beautiful, fashionable clothes.

Florence was very young when she married, and a foreigner, and it seems that she was tolerated rather than embraced by her husband's social circle. Nor does it appear that she was liked by her servants. The gardener objected to Florence's three cats and his wife, Alice Grant, a friend of Alice Yapp's, liked to refer to Florence herself as 'an old cat, always sticking in doors'.

Florence would have had little training or experience in managing a household of servants. The life she had led with her mother had been peripatetic and haphazard, no preparation for any marriage let alone one to a much older man, or for life in the English suburbs. Another woman might have thought twice about letting Mrs Briggs and her sisters come and go as they did. She might also have kept a closer eye on her servants. Unfortunately Florence seems to have been largely unaware of the resentment and jealousy that surrounded her. What she didn't have was a close older female friend or relative who could have given her sound advice. The Baroness didn't really fit the bill. But the support of a trusted friend was exactly what Florence needed when in 1887 she discovered that James had a mistress.

CHAPTER ONE

---

# Domestic Discord

---

James Maybrick's mistress is a shadowy figure and it is unclear how Florence found out about her. She is not named in the documents held in the National Archives, nor was she named at the trial. Christie in *Etched in Arsenic* and Bernard Ryan in *The Poisoned Life of Mrs Maybrick* state that James had three children by his mistress before he married Florence and a further two during the course of his marriage. In *The Last Victim* by Graham and Emmas she is named as Sarah Robertson and it is claimed that James met her when he was working in a shipbroker's office in London as a young man, while she was living with her aunt and uncle in Whitechapel and working as an assistant in their jewellery shop. According to this account she called herself Mrs Maybrick and lived with James in Liverpool, Manchester and Chester, bearing him five children over the years. All accounts state that after he married, James agreed to pay her £100 a year, although as his finances came under pressure this was in fact only honoured sporadically.

Irrespective of who the mistress was, we do know that when

the real Mrs Maybrick found out about her the marriage became troubled. Florence did what many women have done on discovering such news: she stopped sleeping with her husband. About the same time, James's financial circumstances became unstable and Florence was put on an allowance of £7 a week to cover food for the family and staff, household requirements and servants' wages. Unable to manage a budget, she borrowed from moneylenders, and quickly her debts began to mount up. Christie quotes a letter she wrote to her mother in October 1887:

> Whenever the doorbell rings I feel ready to faint for fear it is someone coming to have an account paid, and when James comes home at night it is with fear and trembling that I look into his face to see whether anyone has been to his office about my bills...

To these emotional and financial difficulties were added Florence's anxieties about James's health. In 1877, while in Norfolk, Virginia, James had caught malaria and had been treated with arsenic and strychnine. The Victorians believed these to be aphrodisiacs and James developed a taste for them. Now his wife was beginning to notice his drug habit. In the summer of 1888 she complained to Dr Hopper, his doctor, that James was taking very strong medicine which was affecting him badly. Then in March of the following year she wrote to James's brother, Michael, complaining about the 'white powder' her husband was taking. But when Michael asked him about it James flew into a temper. She also told the children's doctor,

Dr Humphreys (no relation to the Maybricks' cook), that she
thought her husband was taking strychnine. His reply, somewhat offhand and presumably meant as a joke, is recorded in a
supplemental statement he gave prior to the trial in July 1889:
'Well, if he should ever die suddenly call me and I can say that
you have had some conversation about it' (HO 144/1639/A50678).

Christmas brought additional strains. On New Year's Eve
1888, as Christie relates, Florence wrote to her mother, telling
of an argument she had had with her husband:

> In his fury he tore up his will this morning, as he had made me
> sole legatee and trustee for the children in it. Now he proposes
> to settle everything he can on the children alone, allowing me
> only the one third by law! I am sure it matters little to me as
> long as the children are provided for. My own income will do for
> me alone. A pleasant way of commencing the New Year!

It is not surprising given her fraught circumstances that Florence began looking for comfort and distraction. Alfred Brierley
was a cotton man from a wealthy Liverpool family. He was a
friend of James's, 15 years younger, taller and better looking.
It was in November 1888, at a ball held at Battlecrease House,
that their mutual attraction was acknowledged.

The next spring Brierley began accompanying the Maybricks
to the local races. On one occasion he joined them and their
friends the Samuelsons at the Palace Hotel in Birkenhead. In
the evening they played cards and Mrs Samuelson, furious at
being beaten by her husband, said, 'I hate you.' Florence said to

Mr Samuelson, 'You mustn't pay any attention to your wife. I frequently tell Jim I hate him without meaning a word of it' (HO 144/1638/A50678). These words were to come back to haunt her.

Around this time Florence also had an argument with the nanny, Alice Yapp. Coming home earlier than expected one night, she found little Gladys screaming in the nursery three floors up while Yapp chatted with her friends in the kitchen. Florence gave her a good telling off and threatened to fire her if it happened again. A few days later Yapp told Mrs Briggs, who took her side.

Florence Aunspaugh, John's 12-year-old daughter, had stayed with the Maybricks during the summer of 1888. Later, in a letter to Christie written when he was researching his book in the early 1940s, she made this observation: 'Both Mrs Briggs and Nurse Yapp despised and hated Mrs Maybrick and the most pathetic part about it was Mrs Maybrick did not have the brain to realise their attitude towards her.'

In March 1889 Florence embarked on an affair with Brierley. She telegraphed the manager of Flatman's Hotel, 21–22 Henrietta Street, London, and reserved a suite for a week in the name of Mr and Mrs Thomas Maybrick of Manchester. Either she was incredibly foolish or deliberately reckless, because the hotel was a meeting place for cotton brokers from England and the Continent; she had also stayed there once with her mother. To use the family name and choose that hotel for her liaison was hardly the behaviour of someone wanting to keep her actions secret. Perhaps the cavalier way she went about having this affair shows her impulsive nature—after all, she had only taken eight days to decide she wanted to marry James. Maybe she was seeking revenge on him, maybe hoping that this affair could help her escape from an increasingly troubled marriage.

Florence arrived at Flatman's on Thursday 21 March. At 6.30 pm she dined with John Baillie Knight, a distant cousin, and told him that she was seeking a separation from James on the grounds of his adultery and cruelty. Knight recommended a London solicitor.

The following Friday afternoon Brierley arrived, and they dined together that evening in the public dining room. On Saturday morning they were seen together when the waiter brought them breakfast. By Sunday, however, it all seems to have been over. In the affidavit he later swore, Brierley said that they 'parted abruptly' and agreed 'we would not meet again except in public'. The reason he gave was 'chiefly in consequence of my having repeated to her an avowal of my attachment to another lady' (HO 144/1640/A50678). Christie quotes from Sir Charles Russell's brief a claim by Florence that she had been 'momentarily infatuated' and that when Brierley told her about his other attachment she 'had such a revulsion of feeling' that she said she must end their intimacy at once.

Florence spent the rest of the week with Margaret Baillie Knight, John's aunt. She went with Margaret to the solicitors and wrote a letter on their advice to James, seeking a separation on the basis of his adultery and suggesting he pay her an annual income and allow her to continue to live at Battlecrease House with the children.

Before going home she went on a shopping spree. In readiness for the Grand National, which was taking place on 28 March, she bought silk and velvet bags with beetle-wing embroidery of iridescent green spangles, a leather matinée bag containing a scent bottle, new parasols and finally opera glasses. Little did she know that in a relatively short period of time a great many opera glasses would be trained on *her* as she stood in the dock.

Back in Liverpool, James had hired a bus to take himself, Florence and friends including Gertrude Janion, the Samuelsons and Alfred Brierley to Aintree. Brierley bought tickets for the grandstand, and he and Florence went off arm in arm to see if they could catch sight of the Prince of Wales. James was left with Gertrude Janion, who rather liked Brierley herself and was irritated to see Florence swanning off with him. When Florence and Brierley came back it was to find James in a flaming temper, perhaps stoked by the jealous Gertrude. He openly criticized Florence for being gone so long and she said to Mrs Samuelson: 'I will give it to him hot and heavy for speaking to me like that in public' (HO 144/1638/A50678).

Things were now about to become very 'hot and heavy'—but not just for James.

## SEPARATE BEDROOMS

When the Maybricks arrived home a violent argument broke
out which was observed by the servants. Alice Yapp later testified that she heard James say 'This scandal will be all over town
tomorrow' and 'Florie, I never thought it could come to this'
(quotes in this paragraph from HO 144/1638/A50678). Perhaps he
was referring to the affair, perhaps to the separation she was
seeking or perhaps to her debts. At one point in the quarrel
Florence ordered one of the servants to call a cab and James
shouted: 'If you once cross this threshold you shall never enter
these doors again.' She didn't take the cab, but spent the night
in the dressing room off the master bedroom (see plate 2) while
James slept in the dining room.

The following morning Florence went to see Mrs Briggs,
who took her first to her solicitor and then to Dr Hopper. At this
point Dr Hopper takes up the story in the deposition he gave
for the coroner's inquest (HO 144/1638/A50678):

> I visited them at their house and always thought they lived
> happily until March 30th [the day following the argument]. On
> that day Mrs Maybrick called upon me at my house. She had a
> black eye. She told me she wished to have a separation from
> her husband. I advised her not to have one.

Hopper went to Battlecrease House and tried to mediate
between the warring couple. He heard about the quarrel at the
Grand National and Florence's debts: 'She was quite unwilling

at first but I afterwards effected what appeared a perfect reconciliation. During the conversation Mrs Maybrick said she felt some repugnance towards her husband ... I gathered Mr Maybrick was willing to pay the debts.'

In a supplemental statement made in July 1889 Hopper cast more light on the debts: 'They both said she had pawned her jewellery and borrowed from money lenders... She said she had given it to her mother who was hard up' (HO 144/1639/A50678).

In spite of Dr Hopper's efforts another argument broke out. Mrs Briggs had come to stay. According to Mrs Humphreys, the cook, Florence and James argued over her presence in the house. Florence fainted and Dr Humphreys was called out. Christie quotes Mrs Humphreys's statement of what then took place:

> Mrs Briggs kept coming down to the kitchen to me for beer and said she was put out about the quarrel and must have something to keep her up. At about nine she was half undressed and had put on a gown of Mrs Maybrick's which was much too small for her, and she was standing in this condition when Dr Humphreys came and asked who that woman was.

After a week in bed from nervous exhaustion, Florence visited Brierley in secret at his Liverpool home on 6 April — but he gave her no reassurances. Two weeks later James went to London to pay off his wife's debts, which were accruing interest at the eye-watering rate of 60 per cent. Worried as usual about his health, he was persuaded by his brother Michael to see his own doctor, Dr Fuller, who diagnosed hypochondria and indigestion. He prescribed a mild laxative and liver pills known as Plummer's pills, telling James to come back in a week.

Now the lies that Florence had told when planning her liaison were coming home to roost. Because of a mix-up over the forwarding of letters, Margaret Baillie Knight discovered that Florence had lied to her in telling her she had stayed at the Grand Hotel. This led to an anxious correspondence with Florence's mother and then the sending of a sharp letter to Florence:

> The forwarding of the letters was quite an innocent thing. When you were with your friend it did not matter where you were living, but you expressly stated it was the Grand Hotel, and this want of accuracy you see misled us. We are plain people and accustomed to believe what is told us. (HO 144/1638/A50678)

Florence's mother, who was presumably rather better at having secret affairs than Florence herself, had written to her: 'It was ridiculous having your letters addressed to the Grand when you were not there. Your conduct has been indiscreet but I cannot believe you have done wrong' (HO 144/1639/A50678). Dr Hopper recorded that James Maybrick had shown him this communication, which would seem to imply that James was starting to intercept and read Florence's letters.

While her husband was away in London, Florence wrote him a panicky and remorseful letter referring to the men she owed money to (see plate 4):

My own darling Hubby,

The enclosed letter has come this morning from Mr Knightly, nothing from Mr Shore who may be out of town also. I have had a terrible night of it and try as hard as I will to be brave and courageous because Jim thinks I may yet be of comfort to him… I have not sufficient self-respect left to lift me above the depth of disgrace to which I have fallen. For now that I am down I can judge better how very far above me others must be morally. I despair of ever reaching that standard again, although I may receive some of your confidence by living a life of atonement for your and the children's sake alone. Nothing you can say can make me look at my actions but in the most degrading light, and the more you impress the enormity of my crimes upon me the more hopeless I feel of ever regaining my position. I feel as though for the future I must be an eye sore and a perpetual reminder of your troubles and that nothing can efface the past from your memory. My agony of mind last night was just awful and as I promised Jimmy not to take chloral I did not, but I took some lavender instead or bromide, I don't know which or I would have gone mad. Please darling put me out of my pain as soon as you can. I have deceived and nearly ruined you, but since you wish me to live, tell me the worst at once and let it be over… Darling, try and be as lenient towards me as you can. For notwithstanding all your generous and tender loving kindness, my burden is almost more than I can bear. My remorse and self contempt is eating my heart out and if I did not believe my love for you and my dutifulness may prove some slight atonement for the past I should give up the struggle to keep brave. Forgive me if you can dearest and think less poorly of your own wifey.

Bunny

The children are well. I have been nowhere and seen no one.

(HO 144/1639/A50678)

This certainly does not read like the letter of a woman who is intending to poison her husband with arsenic, unless she was being extremely cunning about it. However, at some point in the middle of April, Florence visited Thomas Symington Wokes, a chemist within walking distance of Battlecrease House. The Maybricks had an account there, so Wokes recognized her. She bought a dozen flypapers, remarking that flies had become troublesome in the kitchen, and paid cash for them, asking for them to be delivered to the house. When asked the date of the purchase at Mrs Maybrick's trial the chemist said he could not recall exactly, but that it had been mid-April; he remembered because it was the first lot of flypapers he had sold that spring.

Flypapers had a particularly sinister connotation, especially to the inhabitants of late Victorian Liverpool. In 1884 there had been the famous Flanagan and Higgins trial in which two women had been found guilty of poisoning four people, having soaked flypapers to obtain arsenic. Everyone who worked at Battlecrease House would have known about that famous trial, and so would Florence.

A few days after the purchase, the maid Bessie Brierley noticed flypapers soaking in a wash basin in the master bedroom.

She mentioned this in the kitchen, and Alice Yapp went up to see for herself. No attempt had been made to hide them.

When James returned to the doctor a week later, Dr Fuller found him in better health, changed his prescription and said he would post him a bottle of medicine. On the surface things may have appeared calmer in Battlecrease House, but on 25 April James sat down at work and wrote out a brutally mean-minded will, leaving all his possessions in trust to his brothers Michael and Thomas for the benefit of his children. Florence only got the insurance policies drawn in her name, which were hers anyway. James stated that the furnishings of the house should remain intact for the use of his wife and children and expressed the wish that 'my Widow shall live under the same roof as my children so long as she remains my Widow'.

Presumably he was influenced by the fact that he had had to pay off Florence's substantial debts. Dr Hopper had been told that Florence owed about £1,200 (approximately £100,000 today). Maybe James had borrowed money from Michael and Michael had argued that Florence was too irresponsible to be entrusted with the children's financial future; maybe he had found out about the affair. There is no evidence to suggest that Florence knew anything about this new will.

And so, with the ink drying on the will and the flypapers soaking in the wash basin, the scene was set for the last 16 days of James Maybrick's life.

# CHAPTER TWO

# Alarming Symptoms

The decline of James's health can be traced back to 26 April 1888. On that day he took possession of the box of medicine sent to him from London by Dr Fuller. The following day he vomited and complained of numbness in his limbs. After he had gone out, Florence told Nurse Yapp that he had taken an overdose of the London medicine, and that it contained strychnine and had made him very ill. Despite this he insisted on going to the Wirral races that day on horseback. He got soaked in the rain and then went to supper with friends, where he was embarrassed when his hand shook so much that he knocked over a glass of wine.

The following morning he was very ill and Florence gave him a mustard emetic to make him vomit. She told the cook that he had taken 'another dose of that horrid medicine' (H.B. Irving, *The Trial of Mrs Maybrick*), and called in Dr Humphreys. James told Humphreys that he had felt ill after a cup of tea he had drunk that morning. The doctor thought the problem was indigestion and advised discontinuing Dr Fuller's prescription. He prescribed some dilute prussic acid.

It is perhaps worth saying something about arsenic and flypapers at this point. To prevent flypapers being used for nefarious purposes, they were made with a little bitter-tasting quassia and a brown colouring agent. Soaking one flypaper for a couple of hours would produce a tea-coloured liquid containing 400 mg of arsenic, quite enough to kill. However, to administer the solution it had to be disguised in something that covered the colour and the taste—strong tea, coffee, brandy, sherry or meat juice were ideal for this purpose.

The symptoms of a fatal dose of arsenic start with violent vomiting, followed about 12 hours later by diarrhoea which quickly advances to a state called tenesmus, when the bowel strains ineffectually to evacuate itself. Other symptoms are thirst which is not assuaged by water, a sore mouth and throat, difficulty swallowing and a stomach that becomes extremely tender to the touch. Another notable symptom is muscle spasms, especially in the calves. The afflicted person will slip into a coma and die of heart failure within a couple of days. Lesser doses of arsenic, however, produce symptoms very similar to food poisoning, and this was why the drug was a popular choice for murderers.

In a letter to his brother on 29 April James described his health (see plate 5):

Dear Blucher

I have been very seedy indeed. On Saturday morning [27th] I found my legs getting stiff and useless, but by sheer strength of will shook off the feeling and went down on horseback to Wirral races and dined with the Hobsons. Yesterday morning I felt more like dying than living so much so that Florry called in another Doctor who said it was an acute attack of indigestion and gave me something to relieve the alarming symptoms, so all went well until about eight o'clock I went to bed and had lain there an hour by myself and was reading on my back. Many times I felt a twitching but took little notice of it thinking it would pass away. But instead of doing so I got worse and worse and in trying to move round to ring the bell found I could not do so but finally managed it, but by the time Florrie and Edwin could get upstairs, was stiff and for five mortal hours my legs were like bars of tin stacked out to the fullest extent, but as rigid as steel. The doctor came finally again but could not make it indigestion this time and the conclusion he came to was the Nuxvomica I had been taking. Dr Fuller had poisoned me as all the symptoms warranted such a conclusion I know I am today sore from head to foot and played out completely.

What is the matter with me none of the Doctors can make out and I suppose never will, until I am stretched out cold and then future generations may profit by it if they hold a postmortem, which I am quite willing they should do. (HO 144/1639/A50678)

This letter was not presented at the trial. It was sent to the Home Office afterwards by William Swift, the prosecuting solicitor. On receipt of it a puzzled civil servant wrote to the Home Secretary: 'Mr Maybrick's letter in no way implies his belief that he was being poisoned by his wife' (HO 144/1639/A50678).

But something was obviously the matter with James. Over

the next few days the state of his health fluctuated. Humphreys prescribed bromide of potassium and tincture of henbane; papaine, a vegetable digestive; and iridin, a slight laxative to act on the liver. He also wrote out a diet for him.

On 29 April (about five days after her first purchase) Florence walked into a chemist's in Cressington, a few minutes' walk from home. Christopher Hanson recognized a customer he had known for two years. She asked him to make up a tincture of benzoin and elderflowers and then bought two dozen flypapers which she paid for, again with cash, and took with her.

The next day the cook prepared unsweetened milk and bread for James's breakfast, but he said it had been sweetened and returned it to the kitchen. At work he sent the office boy out to buy some food recommended by Dr Humphreys, Du Barry's Revalenta Arabica invalid food, which was then delivered to Battlecrease House.

That evening Mrs Maybrick went to a masked ball with James's brother Edwin, who had returned from a trip to America on the 25th and was staying with the Maybricks. Alexander MacDougall in his book *The Maybrick Case – A Treatise* quotes Florence writing rather snobbishly to her mother about this, asking for advice about her costume:

> We are asked to a 'bal masque' which, being given in Liverpool and the people provincials, I hardly think likely to be a success. A certain amount of 'diablerie', wit and life is always required at an entertainment of this sort; and as it will be quite a

novel innovation people will hardly know what is expected
of them...

On 1 May the doctor proclaimed James totally recovered. The
cook prepared a jug of Du Barry's food which Edwin was to
take to the office for his brother. Florence came in and asked
the cook to get some paper and string to wrap it up, but when
the cook came back Florence had already wrapped it. At work
James sent the office boy out to buy a basin, pan and spoon.
He warmed the food up but complained that the cook had put
sherry in it, ate very little of it and felt ill afterwards. Traces of
arsenic were later found in the jug.

On the next day, James again took the invalid food to the
office and again he complained of the taste, ate little of it and
felt ill in the afternoon. When the woman who cleaned the office
came to wash the pan she said she noticed black and white par-
ticles in the bottom. That evening James complained of leg pains.

On Friday 3 May Dr Humphreys called and found nothing
wrong with James other than a furred tongue. After a Turkish
bath James went to the office with his Du Barry's food and
sherry, heated it up and consumed all of it. Feeling ill, he rushed
home. There he was sick, and blamed the food and the sherry.
He went to bed, and when Humphreys called he found his
patient suffering from such deep-seated pains in his legs that
he administered a morphine suppository. James was never to
return to his office.

## 'SICK UNTO DEATH'

On 4 and 5 May James continued to vomit. Humphreys suggested Valentine's meat juice instead of the Du Barry's food. On 6 May he prescribed Fowler's solution of arsenic—a common remedy containing a mixture of 1 per cent white arsenic and carbonate of potash—and noted that James was suffering from tenesmus.

While busy nursing (or poisoning?) her husband, Florence maintained contact with Alfred Brierley. It appears that she may have lied to him in suggesting that she had left her husband and that James had been investigating their affair in London. She persuaded Brierley to contact her via John Baillie Knight, and received the following letter from him on 6 May (see plate 8):

> My dear Florie,
>
> I suppose now you have gone I am safe in writing to you. I don't quite understand what you mean in your last about explaining my line of action. You know I could not write, and was willing to meet you, although it would have been very dangerous. Most certainly your telegram yesterday was a staggerer, and it looks as if the result was certain, but as yet I cannot find an advertisement in any London paper. I should like to see you, but at present dare not move, and we had better perhaps not meet until late in the autumn. I am going to try and get away in about a fortnight and think I should take a round trip to the Mediterranean which will take six or seven weeks, unless you wish me to stay in England. Supposing the

rooms are found, I think both you and I would be better away,
as the man's memory would be doubted after three months. I will
write and tell you when I go. I cannot trust myself at present to
write about my feelings on this unhappy business, but I do hope
that some time hence I shall be able to show you that I do not
quite deserve the strictures contained in your two letters. I
went to the D and D [probably dinner and dance] and of course
heard some tales, but myself knew nothing about anything.
And now, dear, goodbye, hoping we shall meet in the autumn.
I will write to you about sending letters just before I go.
  A.B (HO 144/1640/A50678)

Florence then sent a telegram stating somewhat cryptically:
'Recalled owing to Mays critical state, name of street now
known, have secured Henrietta's silence, but left John to
provided [sic] against certain contingencies' (HO 144/1638/A50678).

   John Baillie Knight, the reluctant go-between, was tired of
being embroiled in Florence's intrigues. He now sent her a
furious letter, complaining that it was 'most impolite to tell so
many fibs' to his aunt, and that he was fed up with Florence's
'rather censorious letters'. After claiming a great admiration
for her mother's 'sagacity', he continued:

And now once and for all I am not going to be led into telling
anymore lies or doing any underhand or dangerous missions. I
am quite in the dark now as to what all this mystery is for. And
am I to receive letters for you? Why cannot they be sent to your
own house now? I am obliged to speak what I think because I

am tired of all this scheming which only seems to endanger
your reputation at a most critical time and not to serve any
further end. If I could see that I was serving your interests in
any way I should not perhaps speak as strongly. Besides I have
my own interests to think of and though I daresay you will
think me very selfish, I shall take the utmost care of them...
I should be glad to have a long letter from you in reply to this,
but I will stand no abuse remember... (HO 144/1638/A50678)

On 7 May Florence was sufficiently concerned about her
husband's condition to telegraph Edwin suggesting they get
in another doctor. At midday, Alice Yapp saw Florence on the
landing pouring liquid from one bottle of medicine into another.
That evening Dr Carter, a respected Liverpool toxicologist,
came and examined James, who complained that his mouth was
'as foul as a midden'. Carter's diagnosis was chronic dyspepsia
caused by an irritant in the stomach, and he prescribed antipy-
rine, jaborandi, chlorine water and chlorodine.

## FEMALE SERPENTS

Wednesday 8 May 1889 is one of the most important dates in
the Maybrick case. On this day Mrs Briggs and her sister Mrs
Hughes visited James. According to the *Liverpool Echo* of 13
August 1889, Nurse Yapp said to Mrs Briggs as they arrived:
'Thank God you have come, Mrs Briggs, for the mistress is
poisoning the master. For goodness sake go and see him for

yourself.' She told the women about the soaking flypapers
and also about seeing Florence with the medicine bottles. An
outside nurse was telegraphed for, and three private nurses
named Gore, Wilson and Callery would look after James from
this point. As the same newspaper reported on 14 August, Mrs
Briggs telegraphed Michael in London: 'Come at once, strange
things going on here' (quotes from Graham and Emmas).

When Nurse Gore arrived and took over nursing James,
Florence wrote a letter to Brierley. She gave it to Alice Yapp to
post when she took three-year-old Gladys for her afternoon
walk. This was to prove a fateful decision. Later, under cross-
examination, the nanny claimed that the baby dropped the
letter in the mud and that in the process of transferring the
letter into a new envelope she saw certain words that led her to
read the whole letter. This is what she read (see plate 10):

Dearest
   Your letter under cover to John K. came to hand just after I
had written to you on Monday. I did not expect to hear from you
so soon and had delayed in giving him the necessary instructions. Since my return I have been nursing M. day and night.
He is sick unto death. The doctors held a consultation
yesterday, and now all depends on how long his strength will
hold out. Both my brother-in-laws are here and we are terribly
anxious. I cannot answer your letter fully today, my darling but
relieve your mind of all fear of discovery now and for the
future. M. has been delirious since Sunday, and I know now that

he is perfectly ignorant of everything, even to the name of the street, and also that he has not been making any enquiries whatever. The tale he told me was a pure fabrication and only intended to frighten the truth out of me. In fact he believes my statement although he will not admit it. You need not therefore go abroad on this account, dearest, but in any case please don't leave the country until I have seen you once again. You must feel that those two letters of mine were written under circumstances which must even excuse their injustice in your eyes. Do you suppose I could act as I am doing if I really felt and meant what I inferred then? If you wish to write to me about anything do so now as all the letters pass through my hands at present. Excuse this scrawl, my own darling, but I dare not leave the room for a moment, and I do not know when I will be able to write to you again. In haste

Yours ever,

Florie. (HO 144/1640/A50678)

Yapp marched straight to Edwin and showed the letter to him. When Michael arrived that evening, Edwin showed him the letter too. From this point the brothers took control of the household. Edwin told Nurse Gore that she was to be in total charge of all medicines given to the patient.

The following day Michael told Dr Carter his concerns, having shared them with Dr Humphreys the previous night. Humphreys took away urine and faeces plus some brandy and invalid food that were in the bedroom. Tests on all these proved negative. That evening, Nurse Gore saw Florence take an opened bottle of Valentine's meat juice into her bedroom and, only a minute or so later, try secretly to replace the bottle. This bottle was passed to Michael, who the following day handed it over to Dr Carter. It was later found to contain 38 mg of arsenic.

On 10 May James was weakening. More medicine was prescribed: sulphonal, nitroglycerine, cocaine and phosphoric acid. Michael saw Florence transferring medicine from one bottle to another and confiscated the bottles. He said: 'Florence how dare you tamper with the medicine.' She replied: 'It is on account of the thick sediment which cannot be properly shaken in the smaller bottle.' Later Nurse Callery heard James say to Florence: 'You have given me the wrong medicine again'—an accusation Florence denied. That evening another nurse, Wilson, heard James say to Florence: 'Oh Bunny, Bunny, how could you do it? I did not think it of you.' She replied: 'You silly old darling, don't trouble your head about things' (all quotes in this paragraph from HO 144/1638/A50678). James repeated what he had said three times. These were his last coherent words.

The following afternoon, when Dr Carter arrived, he told Michael that he had discovered a 'metallic irritant' in the Valentine's meat juice and intended to commission further analyses. The bottle was sent off to Dr Edward Davies, an analytical chemist. Carter explained that if James died he would not be able to sign a death certificate. At 8.30 pm James did die. Florence had taken an overdose of chloral that morning and was lying unconscious on the bed in the dressing room.

## SUSPICION BUILDS

At this point Florence takes up the story. Her book *My Fifteen
Lost Years* begins in melodramatic fashion, describing how she
now knew James had died but had been left in the dressing
room largely ignored by the household:

> Slowly consciousness returned. I opened my eyes. The room
> was in darkness. All was still. Suddenly the silence was broken
> by the bang of a closing door which startled me out of my
> stupor… Then a voice, as if a long way off, spoke. I opened my
> eyes in terror. Edwin Maybrick was bending over me as I lay
> upon my bed. He had my arms tightly gripped and was shaking
> me violently. 'I want your keys do you hear? Where are your keys?'

With the brothers now in charge, the children were sent away
and the house was searched. Extraordinary amounts of poison
were discovered; absolutely no attempt had been made to
conceal any of it. In Florence's trunk, which was used to store
towels, they found a chocolate box containing a packet labelled
'Poison' on one side and on the other 'Arsenic. Poison for Cats'.
Also inside the chocolate box were two bottles containing
a white fluid and a brown paper parcel containing a yellow
powder. In two hat boxes (containing James's hats) they found
several small bottles, including a partly full bottle of Valentine's meat juice and a tumbler containing liquid, with a piece
of cloth soaking in the liquid. In the cupboard of an ornate table
they found another bottle with a handkerchief wrapped round

it. Also discovered in Florence's bedroom were some of the incriminating letters and telegrams already mentioned.

Over the next few days 139 jars and bottles, containing a wide variety of different medicines and supplied by 29 different apothecaries, were taken away from the house. A further 26 bottles were found in James's office including 12 locked into his private desk. These ranged from the mundane—'box of corn plasters' and 'blue bottle, Pond's extract Ointment for piles'—to the more startling—'Small bottle containing pills. Labelled poison' from a chemist on Oxford Street (HO 144/1638/A50678). The basin, jug and pan he had used to warm the food brought from home were removed.

Christie quotes a letter written by Charles Ratcliffe to John Aunspaugh in Atlanta on 7 June 1889 (Ratcliffe like Aunspaugh was a friend of the Maybricks). In this letter, which only came to light many years after the trial, Ratcliffe referred to 'female serpents', one of whom he identified as 'old lady Briggs':

> Michael the son-of-a-bitch should have his throat cut. Mrs Maybrick was sick in bed when James died. He had only been dead a few hours when Michael forced her to get up and go with Tom to Liverpool... while she was gone Michael and two policemen searched the house, and in her room they claim to have found quantities of arsenic, thirteen love letters from Edwin, seven from Brierley, and five from Williams.
>
> I always knew the madam was dumb, but I must frankly admit I did not consider her that dumb as to leave her affairs accessible to anyone who choosed [sic] to penetrate... if they

had only found the arsenic in Mrs Maybrick's room as James was such an arsenic dope, I don't think they could have proven anything on her; but finding all those love letters as motive it is going to go hard with her.

Williams is a mysterious figure; according to Christie all that is known about him is that he was a London lawyer. The letters from Edwin and Williams were never produced in court. Maybe the brothers suppressed them or maybe Ratcliffe was simply wrong about this. Whatever the case, Brierley certainly thought that he was her only lover.

Florence was now held under house arrest. On the Sunday after James died the police at Garston were informed that there were suspicious circumstances surrounding the death and Inspector Baxendale was sent to Battlecrease House. He interviewed the Maybricks and the servants and took possession of some of the items which had been discovered. On Monday 13 May the death was reported to the County Coroner, Mr Brighouse, who ordered a post-mortem. This was performed on James's body in the bedroom at Battlecrease House. On hearing that a death certificate had been refused, the superintendent of the county police, Isaac Bryning, went to the house and ordered samples to be taken from the drains. On the following day the County Coroner opened an inquest at Aigburth Hotel to ascertain how James Maybrick had died. A jury of 14 was sworn in, but the inquest was immediately adjourned so that chemical tests on the parts of the corpse could take place.

Florence had been lying ill and weak in bed, unaware of the gathering pace of events outside. Not until three days after James's death was she formally told that she was in custody on suspicion of causing that death. She wrote to her solicitor in America and her mother in Paris. Mrs Briggs, a female serpent if ever there was one, now played a horrible trick on her. Florence did not have enough money to pay for the telegrams or letters, and asked her for help. Mrs Briggs suggested, maliciously, that Florence should write to Brierley; Florence, desperate and presumably still unaware of the woman's hostility towards her, did exactly that (see p. 4). Mrs Briggs took this letter straight to the policeman standing at the front door.

By 15 May, four days after the death, the papers were on the scent and a headline appeared in the *Liverpool Daily Post* announcing 'Suspicious death of a Liverpool Merchant'. The following day, James Maybrick's funeral took place. Florence was not allowed to attend.

On 17 May the Baroness von Roques, a colourful, bellicose character dressed in black silk, arrived in town rather like the cavalry to which her third husband belonged. As reported in the *Liverpool Echo* of 14 August 1889, Michael had finally—four days after the death of his brother—sent her a telegram stating: 'Florie ill and in awful trouble. Do not delay.' This had been followed by two from Florence: 'Jim passed away on Saturday' and 'Come at once serious charges against me' (quotes from Graham and Emmas). At last Florence was to have an ally at her side.

When the Baroness arrived at Battlecrease House, Edwin told her that her daughter was accused of murder and was under house arrest. The Baroness harangued him about why she had not been sent for before. To his rather feeble response that they hadn't known her address, the Baroness, who never lacked for grandiosity, retorted, 'Oh, everyone knew it. "Paris" would have found me.' She then went up to speak to her daughter who was in bed, only to find Inspector Baxendale and Nurse Gore also in the room. Florence said, 'They think I have poisoned Jim.' The Baroness replied, 'Why, if he is poisoned he poisoned himself, he made a perfect apothecaries shop of himself, as we all know' (quotes in this paragraph from MacDougall).

The following day the Baroness went off to see Florence's solicitors, Messrs Cleaver. The kindly Dr Humphreys had informed them of Florence's situation and they had agreed to represent her, although at first they had been refused entry to Battlecrease House by the brothers because they did not have a permit from the police. Even when he gained access on 15 May, Arnold Cleaver was not allowed to speak to Florence in private:

> My communications with her on this occasion were made under great difficulties, being in the presence of a nurse and virtually of a police officer who was at the open door, and were therefore carried out in a low tone and I was unable to make any note in writing of her statement, having been warned that all written statements were examined by the police. (HO 144/1638/A50678)

While the Baroness was in their office they heard that formal charges were being brought against Florence and hurried to the house, arriving to see Florence being removed to Walton gaol, an event observed by the Baroness from the window of an upstairs room into which she had been locked. The following day the papers reported what had happened as 'Extraordinary Magisterial Proceedings' (*Liverpool Daily Post*, 18 May 1889).

Five days after Florence's arrest the brothers removed the contents of the house and put everything up for auction, even the children's toys. They claimed this was from financial necessity, but it directly contradicted the terms of James's will. A contribution of £300 was made towards Florence's defence fund from the money raised, but in the process, evidence crucial to her case went missing.

On 28 May the coroner's inquest resumed. Though Florence was too ill to attend, 40 journalists were champing at the bit, eager to find out the details of what the papers would term 'The Aigburth Poisoning Case'. They were not to be disappointed. At the end of the first day, however, absolutely no evidence had been heard as to the cause of death. This was the whole purpose of the inquest, which was again adjourned—this time until 5 June—to allow James's body to be disinterred and more samples to be sent for testing.

The newspapers went wild. Who cared how James had died? They knew they had a great story on their hands and Florence's letter to Brierley on 8 May was widely reported, as was the disinterring of the body. The *Liverpool Daily Post* wrote a splendidly gothic account of it on 1 June 1889:

> The night was perfectly black and the stillness of the cemetery
> appalling ... there was scarcely anyone present who did not feel
> an involuntary shudder as the pale, worn features of the dead
> appeared in the flickering rays of the lamp held over the
> coffin... What everyone remarked upon was that although
> interred a fortnight the corpse was wonderfully preserved. As
> the dissection knife of Dr Barron pursued its rapid and skilful
> work there was, however, whenever a slight breath of wind
> blew an odour of corruption. The Doctor removed in succession
> his lungs, heart, kidneys, and part of the thigh-bone; coming to
> the head, he cut out the tongue, and, opening the skull removed
> one half of the brain. Each part, as it was removed, was placed
> in a large stone jar which was covered over securely with a
> canvas cloth and sealed with Dr Barron's seal. The job was
> finished as the clock chimed midnight.

At the resumption of the inquest on 5 June (see plate 12) Mrs
Briggs was one of the witnesses, and the letter that Florence
had written to Brierley asking for help when she was under
house arrest was read out. On the next day Dr Edward Davies
of the Royal Institution Laboratory gave evidence that 12 items
removed from the house and office contained arsenic; these
included the bottle of Valentine's meat juice and residues of
dried food found on the jug taken from James's office.

However, he went on to say that very little arsenic had actually been found in James's body. There were unweighable traces
in his intestines and kidneys and only one-fiftieth of a grain (1.3

mg) in part of his liver. This was less than half the quantity which he had found in previous fatal cases of arsenic poisoning. There was some considerable doubt that James had died from arsenic poisoning at all.

The jury, presumably influenced by the enormous quantities of poison found in the house and the evidence of Mrs Maybrick's adultery, nevertheless found by thirteen to one that she did 'wilfully, feloniously, and of her malice aforethought, kill and murder the said James Maybrick' (MacDougall). Florence was now brought into court for the first time and observed that almost all the jury had at one time or another dined in her house. A week later a magistrates' hearing confirmed the verdict of the coroner's inquest and she was committed for trial at the next assizes.

On 28 June, about a month before the trial, Florence wrote from Walton gaol to her mother (the letter is reproduced in *My Fifteen Lost Years*): 'I sincerely hope Messrs Cleaver will arrange for my trial to take place in London. I shall receive an impartial verdict there, which I cannot expect from a jury in Liverpool, whose minds will virtually be made up before any evidence is heard.'

This did not happen. Probably it would have been too expensive, while the Cleavers may also have underestimated the level of hostility towards Florence being generated by the press. However, her solicitors had done something right: they had managed to engage the services of Sir Charles Russell.

Russell was an Irishman and an ex-Attorney-General, a handsome and flamboyant QC who liked to gamble (see plate 15). He had appeared before the Parnell Commission and had just finished successfully defending Charles Stewart Parnell and 65 Irish MPs against the charge of sedition. He was, however, exhausted. His final speech in defence of the MPs had lasted six days. He was also extremely expensive: his usual fee was £500 plus a daily retainer of £100. It was rumoured, however, that 'in the public interest' he had taken a cut in his fees to defend Mrs Maybrick. Maybe the idea of playing a central role in a case which had attracted so much public attention appealed to his vanity. Maybe he was drawn to defending the 'underdog'.

The Baroness set about raising money for her daughter's defence. It was needed not only to pay Sir Charles Russell's fee but because Arnold Cleaver had gone to America to consult with Rowe and Macklin, her American lawyers, who were soon busy tracking down American witnesses to James's drug taking.

From prison Florence wrote to a friend on 27 June: 'God give me strength is my constant prayer. I feel so lonely as if every hand were against me. To think that for three or four days I must be unveiled before all those uncharitable eyes. You cannot think how awful it appears…' (*My Fifteen Lost Years*).

On 26 July Judge Stephen opened the Liverpool Assizes (see plate 14). Sir Leslie Stephen (Virginia Woolf's father) in his biography of his brother, *The Life of Sir James Fitzjames Stephen*, was later to describe him as a 'moralist in the old fashioned sense'. Four years earlier he had suffered from a stroke which had left him with partial paralysis in his right hand. He had recovered but, as his brother later wrote, 'he had made a step downward'. How far downward was to become apparent almost immediately.

The grand jury had to find a 'true bill' against Florence Maybrick for the case to go forward to trial. MacDougall quotes Stephen as talking about 'her adulterous intrigue with a man of the name of Brierley'; Stephen continued, 'if a woman does carry on an adulterous intrigue with another man, it may quite supply—I won't go further [but then he did!]—a very strong motive why she should wish to get rid of her husband.' He then said in error that the letter intercepted by Alice Yapp was written on the Friday and James had died on the Saturday. The letter had in fact been written on Wednesday 8 May, several days before James Maybrick's death.

A true bill was duly found against Florence and the trial date was set for 31 July. On 29 July, while presiding over another matter, the judge was overheard to say in court: 'Sir Charles Russell may very likely wish to plead guilty.' This was reported in the *Liverpool Daily Post* on 30 July under the headline, 'The Judge and the Maybrick Case: Extraordinary Judicial Joke'.

The joke was at the very least indiscreet. It did not reflect well on the neutrality of the judge; nor did it augur well for Mrs Maybrick, who was about to go on trial for her life.

**1** Liverpool Quay in 1875, just a few years before the Maybricks moved to the city. The photograph shows the docks and the shops, both significant in Florence Maybrick's life as the clothes-loving wife of a cotton trader.

# "BATTLECREASE" AIGBURTH

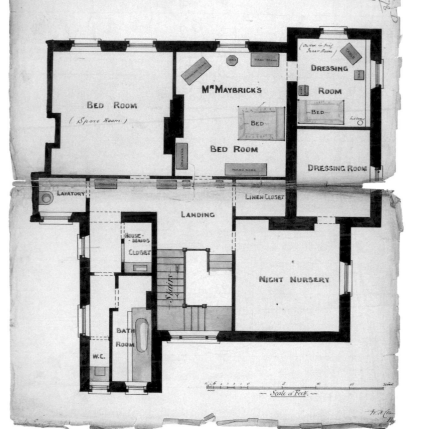

A 50675 D

BED ROOM

( Spare Room )

Mrs MAYBRICK'S

BED ROOM

BED

DRESSING

ROOM

BED

DRESSING ROOM

LAVATORY

LINEN CLOSET

LANDING

HOUSE-
MAIDS
CLOSET

Stairs

NIGHT NURSERY

BATH
ROOM

W.C.

~ Scale of Feet ~

**2** *Left*: Plan of the upstairs floor of the Maybrick's rented home, Battlecrease House, in the Aigburth district of Liverpool. (HO 144/1639/A50678)

**3** *Below*: Exterior view of Battlecrease House.

**4** *Right*: Letter from Florence Maybrick trying to repair her marriage to James, 14 April 1889. (see p. 25; HO 144/1640/A50678)

(Copy)

A 50678 D

29

Liverpool 29th April 188[...]

*"Blucher" is
a name used
or applied
to Michael
Maybrick
by his brother
Wm Fürst

My Dear Michael, Blucher

I have been very very seedy indeed — On
Saturday morning I found my legs getting stiff and
useless but by sheer strength of will shook off the feeling
and went down on horseback to Wirrall Races and dined
with the Hobsons ———— Yesterday morning I felt
more like dying than living so much so that I long called
in another Doctor who said it was an acute attack of
indigestion and gave me something to relieve the
alarming symptoms, so all went on well until about 8
o'clock I went to bed and had lain there an hour by myself
and was reading on my back. Many times I felt a touching
but took little notice of it thinking it would pass away
but instead of doing so I got worse and worse and in trying to
move round touching the bell I found I could not do so but finally
managed it but by the time Florry and Edwin could get
up stairs I was stiff and for two mortal hours my legs were
like bars of iron stretched out to the fullest extent but as
rigid as steel. The Doctor came friendly again but could not
make it indigestion this time and the conclusion he came to
was that the Nux vomica I had been taking under
Dr. Fuller had poisoned me as all the symptoms
warranted such a conclusion I know. I am today sore
from head to foot and played out completely.

What is the matter with me none of the Doctors
so far can make out and I suppose never will until I

**5** *Left*: Letter from James Maybrick to his brother Michael, 29 April 1889. He complains that none of his doctors will know what is the matter with him 'until I am stretched out and cold'. (see p. 29; HO 144/1639/A50678)

**6** *Above left*: Michael Maybrick, who was decidedly hostile to Florence in the Maybrick murder case. He was well known in his own right as a composer and singer, under the pseudonym of Stephen Adams.

**7** *Above right*: Portrait of James Maybrick taken around 1885, just four years before his death.

**8** *Left*: A rather noncommittal letter from Alfred Brierley to Florence, written when her situation was nearing crisis on 6 May 1889. (see p. 33; HO 144/1640/A50678)

**9** *Right*: Portrait of Florence Maybrick registered for copyright on 23 May 1889. (COPY 1/396)

**10** *Far right*: Letter from Florence to Brierley containing the damning words about her husband, 'He is sick unto death', 8 May 1889. (see p. 36; HO 144/1640/A50678)

**11** Part of the seven-page inventory of drugs and other exhibits recovered from James Maybrick's home and office by the police, 14 May 1889. (HO 144/1638/A50678)

Bottles found locked up in Mr. Maybrick's private desk in office, by Mr. Inspector Baxendale, 18 May, 1889.

No. 1. Rye ones compliments.

2. Dark wine bottle. No labels.

3. Old liqueur brandy, vintage 1854

4. Dark mixture from Clay & Abraham's, page 24,216, date 17 June, 1888.

5. Medicine bottle. Thompson & Capper. See copy book, page 467. Contents : Small quantity of water-coloured liquid.

6. Mixture. Clay & Abraham's. Page 246,349. Date 24 April, /89. Medicine bottle, contents : Light yellow-coloured liquid.

7. The gargle. Clay & Abraham's. Page 239,401. Date Nov. 10/87. Light water coloured liquid.

8. Small round bottle from Woke's, Grassendale. No. 02,123. Contents : Light water-coloured liquid.

9. Scent bottle. Contents : small quantity dark brown mixture.

10. Spirits of solvolitile. Edwin G. Easton, Exchange St. East, Liverpool. Contents : Light coloured liquid.

11. Small bottle from Anson's. Contents : Dark brown mixture for Mrs. Maybrick.

12. Small bottle containing pills. Labelled poison. From H. T. Kirby, Newton Street, Oxford Street, London. Nucis Vomacie.

Received.

(Sd.) Edward Davies,

May 18/89.

13. Small bottle, labelled Tincture of Podophyllin.

14. Empty bottle, labelled Clay & Abraham, page 243,868 ; date 25 Oct./88.

15. Empty bottle, containing small quantity red liquid. No label.

16. Small bottle. Drop of sediment. Labelled Clay & Abraham, 243,418—17.9.88.

17. Empty bottle. No cork.

18. Small bottle. Few drops of light-coloured liquid. Written label, " dessert-spoonful."

19. Small bottle containing belladonna pills. Thompson and Capper.

# CHAPTER THREE

# The Eagles Gather

The *Liverpool Daily Post* continued tirelessly to chronicle the Maybrick case. This is how the newspaper began its coverage of the trial on Thursday 1 August 1889:

> 'Wheresoever the carcases there will eagles be gathered together.' There have only been two celebrated trials in Liverpool in the last quarter of a century that have aroused anything like so much interest as the Maybrick Case. Everyone who had admission to the crown court, St George's Hall yesterday as a matter of business — whether he was a juryman, an official or pressman was besieged by applicants for admission by favour. (quotes in this chapter from HO 144/1638/A50678)

Eagles was rather a polite term; vultures would probably have been a more appropriate description for the members of the press who preyed on the case.

Florence was well aware of her notoriety. In *My Fifteen Lost Years* she wrote: 'The press had for two months supplied nourishment in the form of the most sensational stories about me... The excitement ran so high that the Liverpool crowds even hissed me as I was driven through the streets.'

The trial was held at St George's Hall, the home of the law courts; this beautiful neoclassical building, supported by 16 Corinthian columns, had been described by Queen Victoria as 'worthy of ancient Athens'. The Crown Court where Florence was to be tried had seats for four hundred spectators, and competition for these was frenzied. Florence noted that 'Ladies were attired as for a matinee, and some brought their luncheons that they might retain their seats. Many of them carried opera glasses that they did not hesitate to level at me.'

Trumpets announced the arrival of Mr Justice Stephen, six foot tall with mutton-chop whiskers, and dressed in scarlet and ermine robes. He took his seat under a canopy of gold and crimson. Florence was brought up into the blinding sunshine that poured in through the glass roof of the courtroom. She was dressed in widow's weeds and on her head was a tiny crepe bonnet with streamers floating from it. She wore a black transparent veil. Every eye was upon her.

The trial was to last from 31 July to 7 August 1889 (there was no sitting on Sunday 4 August) and included three and a half days of prosecution, one and a half days of defence, then two days of the judge's summing up. Sir Charles Russell was assisted by a prominent Liverpool barrister, Mr Pickford, who had defended Flanagan and Higgins in Liverpool's famous flypaper case. Mr Addison, QC, was the prosecuting counsel. The jury consisted of 12 Lancashire men: three plumbers, a wood turner, a provisions dealer, two farmers, a grocer, an iron-monger, a milliner, a house painter and a baker. Later Florence was to describe them somewhat snootily as ignorant to the point of illiteracy—and they were about to hear a case involving particularly complicated medical evidence.

## DAY ONE: THE PROSECUTION OPENS

On Wednesday 31 July Mr Addison began laying out the prosecution case. He was going to have to prove two things: that James Maybrick had died of arsenic poisoning and that it was Florence who had administered it. He put particular stress on the use of the phrase 'sick unto death' in Florence's letter to Brierley of 8 May and also asked why she had bought two sets of flypapers in such a short period of time: 'It is an extraordinary thing that on Monday [29 April] when her husband was just recovering, she should have bought these flypapers. One asks what she wanted them for and what became of them?'

The prosecution's first witness was Michael Maybrick. By the time Sir Charles had finished with him the court knew that Florence had written to Michael, worried about a white powder her husband was taking (he said he had destroyed the letter); that James had a mistress; and that nothing had been administered to James from the bottle of Valentine's meat juice which had been found to contain arsenic. Also known was the fact that Florence had been prevented from reclaiming the cash box from the bottom of her wardrobe in Battlecrease House.

The next witness was Dr Hopper. He gave evidence about the Maybricks' argument and reconciliation, then Sir Charles asked him about James's health. Hopper confirmed that James was a hypochondriac with a habit of doubling the dose of any medicine his doctor prescribed him: 'I said to him it was a dangerous habit; although he might escape scot-free he would some time do himself great injury.' He went on to say that James had handed him a number of prescriptions that he had been taking in America, which included strychnine and nux vomica. He agreed that they were 'of an aphrodisiac kind', as was arsenic, and confirmed that Florence had spoken to him in a worried manner about her husband's habit of taking a white powder.

Then came Mrs Briggs's testimony. Sir Charles ascertained that she had suggested that Florence write the letter to Brierley asking for financial assistance and then had taken it straight to the police; that she had also thought James very sick on the day Florence wrote that he was 'sick unto death'; that she knew that James had a habit of dosing himself; and that none of the poison found had been hidden in any way. When she stepped down from the witness box a low ripple of disapproval ran through the court. This woman, supposedly Florence's friend, had behaved spitefully and the spectators had not liked what they heard.

Edwin Maybrick was next. Sir Charles established that from the Wednesday before James's death it would have been very difficult for Florence to administer any poison because of the ever-present nurses. He then asked Edwin if to his knowledge his brother took any sort of arsenic. Edwin replied that he did not. Four days later, however, Edwin would be recalled to the witness box because he had handed over to the prosecution a box of pills he had found in the drawer of the wash-stand in his brother's bedroom, at the time the contents of Battlecrease House were being removed. It had been supplied by a chemist in Norfolk, Virginia, and had written on it that the pills contained iron, quinine and arsenic. Edwin had lied.

The two chemists who had sold Florence the flypapers were also called. Sir Charles established that the second set of flypapers was bought at the same time as Florence was having a face lotion of benzoin and elderflower made up, and that arsenic was used as a cosmetic to soften the skin and remove excess hair.

By now the *Liverpool Daily Post*, which had described Florence a little salaciously as 'altogether younger and more attractive in feature and in her slight and well proportioned figure than many of her portraits make her out to be', was coming round to her side: 'Altogether every point in the cross examination told strongly in favour of the accused and the feeling of the auditory as far as could be judged from chance whispers was one of decided sympathy with Mrs Maybrick.'

In only one day of skilful cross-examination, Russell had turned the public opinion in Florence's favour. No wonder that when he left the court that night, he was followed by an immense crowd that cheered him as he entered the North Western Hotel.

## DAY TWO: 'ACQUITTAL PROBABLE'

On Thursday 1 August Alice Yapp was an eagerly awaited witness. She, more than anyone, had been responsible for the suspicions against her mistress. The *Liverpool Daily Post* described her as 'dressed in sober black with a high black hat with ribbon trimmings and a bunch of pink flowers'. She had seemed to relish the inquest, but now she was much more subdued: Mr Addison had to ask her repeatedly to speak up and the clerk recording her evidence kept angrily wagging his quill pen in her direction.

Before beginning his cross-examination Sir Charles nonchalantly took snuff. This gained him the full attention of the court. After ascertaining that Yapp had never been a lady's maid, only a nanny, and thus establishing her as low down in the servants' pecking order, he asked: 'Why did you open the letter?' As Yapp's answers about the muddy envelope failed to convince him, he repeated the question three times, finally thundering: 'On your oath girl did you not manufacture that stain as an excuse for opening your mistress's letter?' Yapp denied it, but Russell had made her appear deceitful and disloyal, thus undermining the character of one of the prosecution's key witnesses.

After testimony from more of the Battlecrease House servants (Bessie Brierley, Mary Cadwallader and the cook, Mrs Humphreys) the next witness was Dr Humphreys, who gave testimony at the end of this day and the beginning of the next.

Over the course of the trial many doctors were called and the evidence became extremely complicated. The problem was that they all differed in their opinion as to whether James had died of arsenic poisoning or not. The difficulty, as far as the prosecution was concerned, was that so little arsenic had been found in James's body—though an additional complicating factor was that arsenic leaves the body very quickly.

Dr Humphreys admitted that if Michael had not come to him with his suspicions he would have given the cause of death as 'acute congestion of the stomach' and would have certified the death as caused by 'gastritis or gastro-enteritis'. When pressed by Sir Charles to 'mention any post-mortem symptom … which is distinctive of arsenic poisoning and which is not also distinctive of gastritis or gastro-enteritis' he could not.

Another interesting statement in Humphreys' testimony revealed that when he tested James's urine and faeces two days before his death, he had found no arsenic. This evidence had not been heard at the inquest or the magistrates' hearing, and was very advantageous to the defence.

At the end of the second day the correspondent of the *New York World* stated that 'Sir Charles put in some sledgehammer work in the way of cross examination today, which caused a great rebound of popular opinion in Mrs Maybrick's favour and makes a disagreement of the jury, if not an absolute acquittal look quite probable.'

## DAY THREE: FEELINGS RUN HIGH

The *Liverpool Daily Post*, covering on 3 August the events of the previous day, reported that 'Mr Brierley, who passed in [to court] was recognised by a few and he was hissed, and the good natured cook Humphreys who sympathised so strong with her mistress, being mistaken for Nurse Yapp was howled at and called a variety of filthy names.'

Dr Carter testified that he was certain that James Maybrick's death was caused by an outside irritant, and by arsenic poisoning, but agreed that his suspicions had not been aroused until a conversation with Michael Maybrick. He also agreed that gastritis could be caused by the ingestion of impure food (for example something James might have eaten at the Wirral races; lobster cheese was mentioned).

Next to give evidence was Dr Barron, who had attended the post-mortem as Florence's representative. He stated that death was due to 'acute inflammation of the stomach probably caused by some irritant poison'—but like Dr Humphreys could not say how the symptoms of death by food poisoning differed from those of death by arsenic poisoning.

Now Dr Edward Davies, the analytical chemist, was called to the witness box. The *Liverpool Daily Post* described his arrival: 'He had to push through the crowd with a huge yellow tin travelling trunk in his arms—this containing the various bottles and jars and other gruesome objects used in the many analyses he had made of the portions of the body.'

A list of items taken from Battlecrease House and James's office was presented (HO 144/1638/A50678) and a copy given to Florence, who started making marks in the margins. Certain of these items had not been produced at the inquest or the magistrates' hearing: Florence's dressing gown, a handkerchief found in the pocket and an apron. Like the items Davies had identified at the inquest, all three contained traces of arsenic.

One interesting point to emerge was that the arsenic in the packet marked 'Arsenic. Poison for Cats' had not been mixed with soot or indigo, as required when arsenic was sold to the public. It had instead been mixed with charcoal. During the trial no explanation was offered by either side as to the origin of this arsenic, but afterwards two accounts emerged. One, that its source was a man named Valentine Blake, has been employed by those who thought Florence innocent; the other, that it was supplied by a Liverpool chemist, is favoured by those who thought her guilty (see pp. 91–4).

On the evening of the third day the Cleavers found their office in pandemonium: letters and telegrams had poured in from all over the country expressing support for Florence.

### DAY FOUR: IN FLORENCE'S DEFENCE

On Saturday 3 August, the three private nurses were first to testify. Then came Alfred Schweisso, a waiter at Flatman's

Hotel, who said that he had seen Florence and Brierley there
together. But the prosecution had saved their most important
witness until last: Dr Thomas Stevenson was a lecturer on
forensic medicine and chemistry at Guy's Hospital, London, and
the official representative of the Home Office and the Treasury
in such trials. Stevenson had received 11 jars containing James
Maybrick's remains removed at the cemetery. He said he had
found no arsenic in the contents of the stomach, in the bile, the
fluid from James's mouth, the spleen, the heart or the lungs. He
had found traces in the liver (76 thousandths of a grain, or 4.9
mg) and the intestines (15 thousandths of a grain, 0.9 mg); these
quantities however were tiny. A fatal dose was two grains (130
mg). Despite this he was adamant that James's death had been
caused by arsenic poisoning. When Sir Charles asked him the
same question he had asked the other doctors, Mr Stevenson
answered: 'There is no distinctive diagnostic symptom of arsenic
poisoning. The diagnostic thing is finding the arsenic.'

But he had found remarkably little.

After lunch Sir Charles Russell began his defence. Aware
that this was a major attraction, the court attendants allowed
more people in than before. Spectators sat on the court steps,
crowded in the aisles and thronged the doorways—and waited
for the great man to speak.

Russell began: 'Gentlemen of the jury, with Mr Pickford I
share the very anxious duty of defending, upon the most serious
charge that can be preferred, this friendless lady in the dock.'

He pointed at Florence who promptly broke down sobbing. After outlining the evidence required in law to find Mrs Maybrick guilty, Russell looked at the Maybrick brothers and said:

> It is an extraordinary fact that, although from Wednesday the 8th May, this lady was deposed from her position of mistress in her own house, no adequate search or enquiry was made. For it does not seem that there was anyone manly enough, friendly enough, honest enough, to go to her and make to her a statement of the charge against her, in order to see whether she had an explanation to offer. The only approach was when she was formally charged by the policeman, which would afford no opportunity except for a mere denial or admission.

Russell went on to state that although arsenic had been found in Battlecrease House there was no evidence of Florence acquiring poison other than the flypapers.

He then asked the judge whether she could make an informal statement in evidence for the defence. This was not allowed by the English legal system but Judge Stephen was known to think that it should be. He gave permission for Florence to address the court, although no one, including her legal team, could be consulted about her statement and she was not to write it down. It was agreed that she would speak after all the defence witnesses had been called (although this meant that defence witnesses could not be called to corroborate anything she said).

Finally, Sir Charles addressed the matter of Florence's affair with Brierley:

I refer to that dark cloud that passed over her life and rests upon her character as a woman and a wife. But I would entreat you not to allow any repugnance resting in your minds against a sin so abhorrent as that to lead you to the conclusion, unless the evidence drives you irresistibly there, that, because a wife has forgotten her duty and faithfulness to her husband, she is to be regarded as one who deliberately and wickedly will seek to destroy his life.

It was a hot afternoon. Sir Charles sat down, wiped his face and theatrically took snuff. The first defence witnesses could now be called. The thrust of the defence was that there was reasonable doubt that James Maybrick had died of arsenic poisoning, and that there was an explanation for the arsenic found in his body: Maybrick was a drug addict and known to dose himself.

The first three witnesses, Mr Nicholas Bateson, Captain Robert Thompson and Thomas Stansell, had all known James in America and gave evidence about his drug taking. Stansell, for example, had been a servant of Maybrick between 1877 and 1881. He described how he had bought James arsenic which had been taken in beef tea. Then came an English witness, Edwin Garnett Heaton, a chemist in Liverpool for 37 years until his retirement a year before. He had recognized James Maybrick's picture in the newspaper as being that of a customer he had provided with a 'pick-me-up'. James had then changed the tonic to include *liquor arsenicalis*. Over time the number of arsenic drops had increased from four to seven, and James had stopped in to get it from two to five times a day.

The prosecution sought to undermine this witness by pointing out that there was no evidence on his books of Maybrick being a customer, and that recognizing someone's picture in the paper was insufficient proof. In fact there *was* proof that James was Heaton's customer: on the list of drugs present in court was a bottle taken from the locked drawer of James's desk in his office (see plate 11). The label stated: 'Spirits of solvolatile [sic]. Edwin G. Easton, Exchange St. East, Liverpool. Contents: Light coloured liquid' (HO 144/1638/A50678). A policeman had written down the name incorrectly as Easton, not Heaton; no one saw the connection.

Other witnesses at this stage were Dr Drysdale, who testified to James's hypochondria and drug taking (including the consumption of nitro-hydrochloric acid, strychnine and hydrate of potash); William Thomson, who had seen James at the Wirral races and heard him say that he had taken a double dose that morning; and John Thompson, a wholesale druggist, who had employed one of Maybrick's cousins and suspected him of supplying James with drugs.

Now the defence called Dr Charles Tidy, its most weighty medical witness. Like Dr Stevenson, he was an analyst for the Home Office and an Examiner of Forensic Medicine, and had assisted at forty post-mortems involving arsenic poisoning. When asked by Sir Charles about the cause of James's death, he said 'That it is due to gastro-enteritis of some kind or another but that the symptoms of the post mortem distinctly point away from arsenic.'

It was with this telling evidence in favour of the defence that the fourth day of the trial ended.

## DAY FIVE: MRS MAYBRICK'S STATEMENT

Monday 5 August was a general holiday, so people flooded in even greater numbers to St George's Hall. The session began with yet more doctors. Both Dr Macnamara, a professor at the Royal College of Surgeons in Ireland, and Dr Paul, thought James had died from gastro-enteritis caused by a combination of factors: a stomach weak from drug taking, an error of diet and a soaking at the Wirral races.

The final witnesses for the defence were a chemist, Hugh Lloyd Jones, who stated that he had known women buy flypapers for cosmetic reasons; James Bioletti, a hairdresser, who said that arsenic was known as a depilatory; and Sir James Poole, a former mayor of the city, who said that at the Palatine Club James had told him: 'I take poisonous medicines.' To this Sir James had replied: 'How horrid. Don't you know, my dear friend, that the more you take of these things the more you require, and you will go on till they carry you off?'

The defence had done well. It had supplied sound medical evidence disputing that James died of arsenic, and plenty of proof that he was a hypochondriac and drug addict, which could explain the arsenic in his body. And the evidence that arsenic was used by women as a cosmetic and depilatory provided an alternative explanation for Florence's purchase of flypapers.

Now Florence stood up to make her statement. This was what the crowd of spectators had been waiting for; they had been watching her for five days. What would she say? As Florence stood and wiped her eyes with her handkerchief, everyone in the courtroom strained to see her. She began by saying that the flypapers had been bought as a cosmetic:

> Before my marriage and since I have been in the habit of using a face wash prescribed for me by Dr Greggs of Brooklyn. It consisted of arsenic, tincture of benzoin, elderflower water, and some other ingredients. This prescription I mislaid last April and as I was suffering from slight eruption of the face I thought I should like to make a substitute. I was anxious to get rid of this eruption before I went to a ball on the thirtieth of that month.

She claimed that as a young girl in Germany she had known her friends to make up such a face wash. She then explained about the bottle of meat juice:

> On Thursday night, the 9th May, after Nurse Gore had given my husband beef tea, I went and sat beside him. He implored me to give him his powder which he had referred to early in the evening, and which I had declined to give him. I was terribly anxious, miserably unhappy, and his evident distress utterly unnerved me. He had told me the powder would not harm him, and that I could put it in his food. I then consented.

> When I found the powder, I took it into the inner room, with the beef juice, and in pushing through the door I upset the bottle and in order to make up the quantity of fluid spilled, I added a considerable amount of water.

Florence went on to say that when she returned to his room James was asleep; she put the bottle (of juice and arsenic) out of sight because she did not want him to take it, and later Michael removed the bottle. She concluded: 'I have only to add that for the love of our children, a perfect reconciliation had taken place between us, and that on the day before his death I had made a full and free confession to him, and received his entire forgiveness for the fearful wrong I had done him.' As Florence sank back into her chair she was offered smelling salts.

Sir Charles immediately asked the judge if he could bring witnesses to corroborate what Florence had said. Presumably these would have been her solicitors, the Cleaver brothers. But the judge replied that as the law stood he could not allow this. So Sir Charles had to proceed straight to the closing statement for the defence. If he had known that Florence had put something in her husband's food, it seems extraordinary that he let her admit it. It had not made his task any easier. Nurse Gore had not actually seen Mrs Maybrick tamper with the Valentine's meat juice, she had merely suspected it. Even though it was agreed that James had not drunk from the bottle in question, Florence's statement had not left a good impression on the jury.

Sir Charles took snuff, shuffled his papers, and launched

into his closing statement. He portrayed James Maybrick as a man suffering from chronic dyspepsia and hypochondria and with a habit of dosing himself with all kinds of drugs. In dealing with Florence's adultery he said: 'This lady fell. She forgot her self-respect. She forgot her duty to her husband...' He then addressed the Victorian double standard when it came to these matters. 'In a man such faults are too often regarded with toleration, and they bring him often but few penal consequences. But in the case of a wife, in the case of a woman, it is with her sex the unforgivable sin ... because she sinned once, is she therefore to be misjudged always?'

He went on to pour scorn on the idea that Florence would have bought flypapers from two chemists who knew her by name if her intention had been to poison her husband, and also to ask why, if she had murdered James, there had been no attempt to hide all the poison that was lying around the house. 'You will say whether if such a woman had the nerve and fibre enough to plan such a murder as this—cold, deliberate—she would not also have had the instinct of self preservation...'

He reminded the jury that they must be absolutely sure that arsenic poisoning had taken place at all, and then went on to deal with Florence's statement. This, not surprisingly, was the weakest part of his speech. What could he possibly say to counter Florence's damaging admissions?

I will not enlarge on it [her statement]. I leave it to speak with such effect on your ears and hearts as the circumstances under

which it was delivered and the way in which it was delivered
and the tone in which it was delivered and the inherent prob-
abilities of the delivery itself will suggest to you what ought to
be its proper and legitimate result.

Presumably he was advising the jury to look beyond Florence's
words to see the true fact of her innocence, but his phrasing
probably bemused the jury just as much as all the contradictory
medical evidence. He concluded with the standard challenge to
the jury: 'can any one of you with satisfied judgment and with
safe conscience, say that this woman is guilty?'

Mr Addison now put the closing arguments of the prosecution. He portrayed Florence as a liar, using as proof the evidence
of her various letters to book the rooms at Flatman's Hotel, and
placed great emphasis on the purchase of two sets of flypapers
so closely together. Stressing the use Florence had made in her
letter of the expression 'sick unto death', he claimed that she
was 'consummately cunning'. Then he came to her statement,
stating disingenuously: 'I can hardly help having a feeling of
regret that the terrible statement which has been made today
should have been made.' He went on to ask why, if Florence had
been so worried about the powder her husband had been taking,
she had put it in his meat juice: 'Was it possible she could have
innocently done this thinking it would not do him any harm?'

Mr Addison finished: 'If she be guilty … we have in this
investigation brought to light a very terrible deed of darkness
and proved a murder founded upon profligacy and adultery and

carried out with hypocrisy and a cunning which have been rarely equalled in the annals of crime.'

Meanwhile, outside the court, Florence's statement was telegraphed in full to the *New York World* and a reporter was sent to track down Dr Greggs in Brooklyn (whom Florence had claimed made up a face wash for her). Asked about Florence Maybrick, Dr Greggs said: 'All I know about Mrs Maybrick is that she called upon me to prescribe something for her complexion, which I did.' When asked by the reporter, he confirmed that there had been arsenic in the prescription.

## DAY SIX: THE SUMMING UP

On Tuesday 6 August Russell was not in court, having taken another case. Judge Stephen seems to have managed a degree of neutrality in his presentation of the evidence to the jury, though there were aspects of the summing up which puzzled legal onlookers. He referred to newspaper cuttings instead of his own notes, and muddled dates, saying that the flypapers had been bought in March, not April. He also referred to 'a fatal dose' being administered on the Friday, hardly a neutral statement, and described Captain Thompson, one of the defence witnesses, as 'foolish'. At one point he confused Dr Stevenson with Dr Tidy: the two doctors held directly opposing views.

After lunch, as Mr Addison lay with his head on his desk, snoring, perhaps from too heavy a lunch, the judge embarked on a long speech about the cause of James Maybrick's death. There is no doubt that the medical evidence was complex and contradictory, but it was his job to sum up the evidence as best he could for the jury. The following paragraph shows that he was unable to do so:

> The evidence of a certain number of medical men is, 'I think he died of arsenic poisoning,' or 'I don't think he died of arsenic poisoning but of gastro-enteritis, caused by the administration, or, at any rate, caused by something capable of causing gastro-enteritis but not necessarily arsenic,' and in some instances 'probably not arsenic.' These parts may be passed over as more fit for medical jurisprudence than for a jury engaged upon the administration of criminal law.

Later, talking about the disagreement of various doctors over the question of how long arsenic stayed in the body, the judge rubbished the medical profession in general:

> A celebrated physician said that a physician spent his time putting drugs of which he knows little into a body of which he knows less. This is one of those pointed sayings, but there is truth at the bottom of it. It cuts against the prosecution, and it cuts against the defence, and it lowers the degree of assurance with which we receive medical evidence.

None of this was very helpful to a jury faced with the task of considering the medical evidence, but at least at this point the judge remained relatively neutral. On the second day his neutrality was to completely disappear.

That night the judge sharing lodgings with Judge Stephen woke up to find him pacing round the room saying, 'That woman is guilty.' It was certainly what he was to express in no uncertain terms to the jury the following day.

## DAY SEVEN: THE VERDICT

*The Reviews Reviewed* described the behaviour of Judge Stephen on 7 August as follows: 'he came into the court and charged horse, foot and artillery upon the wretched and forlorn woman in the dock.' The judge began by getting confused over the quantity of arsenic found in James Maybrick's intestines, talking of 'one fifty-three thousandths' of a grain instead of 15 thousandths. He then rambled obscurely: 'I cannot convey anything to enable you to attach meaning to figures representing such very small quantities. The globules of blood in a man's body are so small that there are more than a billion, but really that conveys no idea whatever to our minds.'

Before long he addressed the various letters and telegrams that had been found in Battlecrease House, quoting from the letters sent by John Baillie Knight and his aunt and claiming that these showed Florence was a liar. They had not, however, been produced as evidence, and he should not have read from them. He asked who 'John' was and began to read from the letter written by Florence to Alfred Brierley on 8 May, speculating that John was another man with whom Florence was carrying on an affair. 'Here are different persons connected with her charging her with living in a maze of falsehoods.' He then began reading out the Brierley letter again, interposing his own comments. He also said that he doubted Florence and James had been reconciled as Dr Hopper had claimed.

On the subject of flypapers, Judge Stephen was caustic. Why had the defence brought no evidence to support Florence's claims about their innocent purpose, for example from Dr Greggs? Why hadn't her mother given evidence of her daughter's use of a cosmetic face wash that included arsenic? And why hadn't witnesses been brought from Germany to confirm Florence's claim that her childhood friends also used arsenic as part of their beauty routine? This omission could not have arisen from shortage of funds, because the defence had found the money to bring witnesses from America.

After lunch things were no better. Judge Stephen made a further error of fact, saying that one of the bottles held in evidence had contained 94 per cent arsenic when the percentage cited in court was actually two and 94 one-hundredths, or 2.94 per cent. Then he launched into a tirade which ended: 'It is easy enough to conceive how a horrible woman, in so terrible a position, might be assailed by some terrible temptation.' The judge seemed to be asking for the jury to reach a verdict of guilt based on motive rather than the facts. By the time he eventually finished with Florence Maybrick he had been speaking for 12½ hours. The jury was out for only 38 minutes.

In her memoir Florence wrote: 'When I stood up to hear the verdict I had an intuition that it was unfavourable. Everyone looked away from me, and there was a stillness in court that could be felt.' After the foreman of the jury had pronounced her guilty Florence described what happened next: 'A prolonged "Ah!" strangely like the sighing of wind through a forest sounded through the court. I reeled as if struck a blow and sank upon a chair.'

When she was asked if she had anything to say, she responded: 'My Lord, everything has been against me. Although evidence has been given as to a great many circumstances in connection with Mr Brierley, much has been withheld which might have influenced the jury had it been told. I am not guilty of this crime.' She then slumped into her chair and sobbed.

The judge put on a black silk cap and sentenced her to death. The trial had concluded in the way that his instincts had dictated from the start. But public opinion was outraged at Florence's fate (see plate 13). As *The Times* reported the next day:

> A large mob had assembled outside the court and showed much
> indignation at the verdict. The counsel and witnesses were
> hooted and even Mr Justice Stephen had to drive away guarded
> by police. On the other hand as the van containing the prisoner
> and guarded by mounted police passed out of the courtyard,
> loud cheers were raised.

As the law stood, three Sundays must pass before the condemned could be hanged: the date for the execution was set for 26 August. Florence's friends had 18 days to save her.

# CHAPTER FOUR

# The Gallows Beckon

Things looked bleak for Florence. In 1889 there was no criminal court of appeal, and this fact—as well as the outcome of the trial—inspired strong public reaction. Ryan quotes from an article by the London correspondent of the *New York Times*, writing shortly after Florence's conviction: 'The state of English law practice in murder cases is simply shocking. Here there is no appeal from capital conviction. A man may secure a new hearing over a case which involves a sixpence but when it is a question of his life it is rigorously denied him.'

The only possible approach was an appeal to the Home Secretary, who could in turn make a recommendation to the Queen for a pardon. On 7 August Sir Charles Russell went straight back to the North Western Hotel and wrote the following letter to Home Secretary Henry Matthews:

> I am sorry to say it will be necessary for you fully to consider this case.
>
> Against her there was a strong case undoubtedly of the means being within reach to poison her husband and of the

Foreman of the Jury · Mr. A. G. Steel Counsel for Mrs. Maybrick · Mr. Edwin Maybrick · Mr. Michael Maybrick · Alice Tapp, Nurse · Humfries, Cook · Dr. Carter

Mr. Pickford, Q.C., Counsel for the Defence · Mr. Brighouse, Coroner · Supt. Bryning Prosecutor · Inspector Baxendale

THE SCENE AT THE CORONER'S INQUEST ON THE DEATH OF THE LATE MR. MAYBRICK.

**12** Engraving (detail) of the coroner's inquest on 5 June 1889, from an illustration in the *Graphic*. Many of the principals were present including Alice Yapp and Michael Maybrick.

# THE MAYBRICK MYSTERY.

## GREAT OUTBURST OF POPULAR INDIGNATION IN LIVERPOOL.

### JUSTICE STEPHEN DEPARTS AMID A STORM OF GROANS

### MRS. MAYBRICK CHEERED BY THE CROWD.

### IMPORTANT STATEMENT BY THE PRISONER

### EFFORTS FOR REPRIEVE.

### WHO AND WHERE IS "JOHN"?

#### THE SCENE AFTER THE VERDICT.

Immediately upon the prisoner's disappearance from court a remarkable ebullition of feeling took place. Hisses were heard, not in a volume, but singly, and in various parts of the court. They could only be assumed to be directed at the jury, who stood in their box awaiting their discharge. Mr. Justice Stephen was standing by his seat; if he heard the sounds he made no remark upon them, but, addressing the jury, he tendered them the thanks of their country for their discharge of the awful duty which had been imposed upon them, and intimated that, following precedent, he had directed that for five years they should be relieved of further duty as jurors.

The members of the jury, several of whom had been deeply affected during the dread proceedings that followed upon their verdict, then retired.

#### MRS. MAYBRICK'S DEMEANOUR AFTER SENTENCE.

The demeanour which she recovered when she left the dock, with her life forfeited to the law, she preserved to the end. Waiting in the cell below, she was outwardly a spectacle of that calmness, almost stoical, which, even under such an ordeal, she had been able, except for a few moments, to preserve. It was the same when in the gloomy passage below the court she entered the ominous-looking prison van.

#### HOW SIR CHARLES RUSSELL RECEIVED THE VERDICT.

As soon as the verdict was given Sir Charles Russell, who had several times in the course of the observations of the judge shaken his head in dissent, hurriedly left the court, evidently under the influence of deep emotion. He hurried along the corridor to a private room, and was followed by Mr. Cleaver, the solicitor for the defence, and others. Many kindly expressions were sent to him from other members of the Bar, and a proposal was at once put on foot for a petition from members of the Bar generally in favour of a commutation of the sentence.

#### A JUDGE DOUBTED THE REPORT "GUILTY."

It is said that, in common with Sir Charles Russell and most of the counsel engaged at the Assizes, Mr. Justice Grantham, sitting in the Nisi Prius Court, received the news of the verdict with incredulity, and sent his clerk round to ascertain if it was really true that the verdict was "Guilty."

#### A BOUQUET PREPARED FOR MRS. MAYBRICK.

A number of ladies had a magnificent bouquet ready to present to Mrs Maybrick, believing her acquittal to be certain, and one of them actually saw Mr. Shuttleworth at lunch time, and asked if the bouquet might be presented across the dock in the case of an acquittal. The Clerk of the Arraigns was much shocked at the proposal, and said he was surprised the request had been made.

#### MR. BRIERLEY.

During the summing-up a sensation was caused in court by the judge giving an intimation that Mr. A. Brierley should be sent for. The belief was that his lordship, exercising his power, might very likely ask Mr. Brierley to be called

**13** *Left*: Headlines from the *Pall Mall Gazette* reporting the shocked reaction to the Maybrick verdict, 8 August 1889. (HO 144/1638/A50678)

**14** *Above*: Sir James Fitzjames Stephen, the judge who conducted the Maybrick trial and was—unfortunately for Florence—a 'moralist in the old fashioned sense'.

**15** *Below*: Sir Charles Russell, who conducted Florence's defence and was an indefatigable campaigner for her freedom, in 1894.

**16** *Right*: Seven-page memorandum from Charles Russell to the Home Office making the case for Florence Maybrick's reprieve, 14 August 1889.
(see p. 74; HO 144/ 1638/A50678)

FLORENCE MAYBRICK.

## Memorandum

The Questions.

There were two Questions.
(1) Was it proved beyond reasonable doubt that the deceased died from arsenical poisoning ? - and if so
(2) That the prisoner criminally administered that poison ?

1. Arsenical poisoning ?

(1) Arsenical poisoning :

Although Dr. Humphries was in attendance from the 28th April and Dr. Carter from the 7th May until the 11th May, when the deceased died, the idea of arsenical poisoning did not occur to either of them until the use of arsenic was first suggested to them - namely on the night of Wednesday the 8th of May or Thursday the 9th of May. Indeed Dr. Humphries would have been prepared to give a certificate of death from natural disease had he not been informed of the arsenic being found in a small bottle of meat juice.

Symptoms.

As to the symptoms it was agreed by the expert Witnesses on both sides that they were symptoms of gastro enteritis that is inflammation involving both stomach and intestines. For the prosecution it was said that this disease was set up by arsenic : for the defence that three principal symptoms of arsenical poisoning were absent namely, violent diarrhœa - pain in the pit of the stomach increased on pressure, and, cramps in the calves of the legs. It was also pointed out that although vomiting was present it was not excessive. Further, while it was admitted that one or other of these symptoms might be absent in a case of arsenical poisoning, the absence of so many of the principal ones in conjunction was considered unaccountable. Indeed Dr. Tidy expressed the strong opinion that the symptoms taken all together "pointed away from" arsenical poisoning.

Appearances Post mortem.

It was admitted by the prosecution that the Post mortem appearances were such as might follow death from severe gastro enteritis : but it was urged that gastro enteritis was not ideo-pathic and that there was no cause other than arsenic to be suggested. On the other hand, the experts called for the defence said that there was one mark characteristic of arsenical poisoning which was absent, namely, a petichious (fleabitten) condition of the stomach, and that as it was admitted that the deceased had been in the habit of drugging himself and had for years complained of a deranged stomach, a wetting such as that suffered on the 27th April at Wirrall Races and any error in diet would be sufficient to set up the gastro enteritis. Further the deceased told Dr. Humphries that on the morning of the 27th

1

**17** *Below left*: Queen Victoria, who was 'inflexibly convinced of Mrs Maybrick's guilt'. (COPY 1/134)  **18** *Below right*: Black-edged response from Balmoral to an American petition for Florence's reprieve, 2 October 1891. It reads: 'The Queen entirely approves and agrees with Mr Matthews on the case of Mrs Maybrick'. (HO 144/1639/A50678)

**19** *Opposite*: Page from Alexander MacDougall's petition on Florence's behalf to the Home Secretary Sir Matthew White-Ridley, 31 December 1895. It details the aggressive course of treatment that Doctors Carter and Humphreys prescribed for James Maybrick in his dying days. (HO 144/1640/A50678)

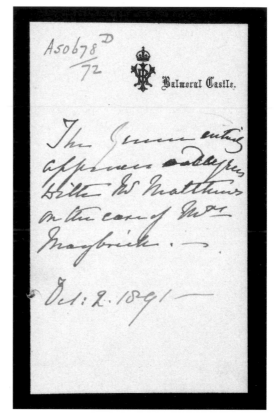

| May 7th con: | | | | Prescribed by. |
|---|---|---|---|---|
| " " | Arsenic discontinued because it burned patient's throat. | | | Dr.Humphreys. |
| " | Sanitas to wash mouth. | | | " " |
| " | Antipyrine | | | Dr.Carter & Dr.Humphreys. |
| " | Tincture of Jaborandi | " " | " " | |
| " | Chlorine water to wash mouth | " | " | " |
| " | Chicken broth, Milk, and Lemon water, Neave's Food. | " " | " " | |
| " 8th. | Jaborandi. | | | " " |
| " | Antipyrin. | | | " " |
| " 9th. | Bismuth | | | " " |
| " | Opium Suppository. | | | " " |
| " | Bismuth (Double dose) | Dr. Carter & Dr.Humphreys | | |
| " | Sulphonal . | " " | " " | |
| " | Cocaine. | " " | " " | |
| " | Valentine's Meat Juice (given him by Nurse Gore) | " " | " " | |
| " 10th. | Cocaine | " " | " " | |
| " | Nitro-Glycerine. | " " | " " | |
| " | Phosphoric Acid. to wash mouth. | " " | " " | |
| " | Nutritive Suppository | " " | " " | |
| " | Glycerine. to wash mouth (Nurse Gore) | " " | " " | |

May 11th.  Death from exhaustion resulting from gastro-enteritis.

That he should die from exhaustion resulting from gastro-enteritis after a fortnight of such treatment by these two Doctors who had thus, with almost daily change, been attacking this man's stomach with this variety of depressing drugs and irritant poisons, cannot be a matter of surprise to anyone, expecially when it is considered that on the 4th of May he was ordered to

**20** *Above*: Florence's facewash prescription including arsenic. It would have been crucial evidence at her trial, proving her use of arsenic as a cosmetic, but was lost until Baroness von Roques recovered it in 1893/4 when it fell out of Florence's bible. (HO 144/1639/A50678)

**21** *Right*: Report on Florence's health from the governor of Aylesbury prison, 27 July 1898. By this time Florence seemed to have been part-reconciled to her fate after a period of unrest. (HO 144/1640/A50678)

Office No.16203     A50678/320

H.M. Convict Prison,

Aylesbury,

27th July, 1898.

Reg. P.29 Florence C. Maybrick.

Liverpool Assizes 25 July 1889

Murder - Life (commutation of Death Sentence)

Gentlemen,

In accordance with the instructions contained in the accompanying letter No.16203/216 dated the 23rd inst: asking for a full report upon the condition of the above-named Prisoner, I beg to state that at the present time her health is fairly good, and she is free from any organic disease. Her weight - 112 lbs - is exactly the same as on her reception into Prison.

Although imprisonment does not appear to have had any injurious effect upon her general health, it appears to have had the effect of making her, at times, morose and bad tempered, and inclined to make herself very disagreeable to her fellow Prisoners. Her mental condition has, however, decidedly improved during the past twelve months, for whereas she then professed inability to employ herself in any way, either by doing needle-work or reading, she now not only amuses herself by reading, but is fairly industrious both at knitting and needle-work.

I am of opinion that she will not be injuriously affected by further imprisonment.

I have the honour to be,

Gentlemen,

Your obedient Servant,

(sd) George E. Walker

Governor & M.O.

The Directors

# A MOTHER'S ANGUISH.

## Woman Who Was Central Figure in Great Poison Drama of the Nineties.

## CAME FOR RECONCILIATION, BUT—

### By a Special Representative.

*Unknown to anyone save her solicitor and a few personal friends, Mrs. Maybrick, the central figure in one of the most sensational poison dramas of the last decade of last century, has just concluded a brief visit to England, and the only interview she gave during her stay is published exclusively below :—*

SAD-FACED, gentle-voiced, with hair turned to silver, the Mrs. Maybrick of to-day is but a shadow of the striking-looking woman who made a lasting impression on those who saw her in the dock at Liverpool, 37 years ago, fighting for her life against the mass of circumstantial evidence linking her with the murder by arsenical poisoning of her husband, a wealthy Liverpool stockbroker.

"I feel death's shadow over me, and I have come back with one object only, to effect a reconciliation with members of my family, if that be possible. To that end I am trying to clear myself of the charge of murder of which I was convicted and sentenced to death."

This statement was made to me at my first meeting with the once notorious woman. Later, when she had made overtures through friends, she confessed sadly that her hopes of reconciliation were dead. "It is bitterness worse than death," she said.

**Mrs. Maybrick**

"All the years that have passed since that terrible day when I heard the verdict of guilty I have longed for my children, who were but babes at the time, and the mother hunger in my heart was so strong that I felt I must make this journey now in the hope of seeing them.

## "BROKEN MY HEART."

### Terrible That Children Should Think Me Guilty.

"The knowledge that it has been in vain has almost broken my heart. M---

## CHEMIST'S EVIDENCE.

### "Remembers Having Sold Poison To My Husband."

"The charge against me was that I had administered arsenic taken from fly papers to my husband, and much was made of the fact that this was the only way in which the poison could have come into the house. At the time my mind was in such torment that I could not think clearly, but thinking over the case since I have recalled facts that suggest my husband was in the habit of taking arsenic in fairly strong doses.

"There is also the evidence of a Liverpool chemist who remembers having sold the poison to my husband some time before the death. I believe this evidence was brought forward after the trial, and had weight with the Home Secretary in advising a reprieve for me.

"In addition," she went on, "there is the new light that science can shed on the amount of arsenic likely to be found in a body after a natural death. I have been told by one of the most

respected lawyers in England that, had what science now states about arsenic being found in most bodies after death been known, I should have been acquitted by the jury instead of being convicted on a presumption that science now declares to be false."

Having given all the assistance she can for this new investigation of the case, Mrs. Maybrick has returned to her American home, where she lives the life of a recluse.

"If the new inquiries bear fruit and produce the evidence necessary to establish my innocence, I shall return to England to make one last attempt at reconciliation, for death without the forgiveness of my children for all the unhappiness I have brought them through my folly would be terrible.

## PAYING FOR LOVE.

### "Bitterly Have I Repented

existence of a motive but there was no <u>direct</u> evidence of admin-
istration by her. But further; but a small quantity of arsenic
was discovered in the body after death and <u>none</u> in the
stomach, bile, heart, spleen.

The symptoms—all were agreed—were those of gastro-
enteritis; but while the witness for the prosecution attributed it
to arsenical poison a very strong body of evidence was given for
the defence that it was not so.

The woman had been unfaithful to her husband and I am
afraid this fact and her subsequent improper letter to her para-
mour unsettled Justice Stephen's ordinarily fair judgment.

In a long experience I never heard any summing up which
gave a jury less chance of differing from his clearly conveyed
adverse view.

Indeed he seemed to have told the jury to consider the case
as a whole and not dispute its consideration; and thus he
appears to have suggested to them that even if the <u>cause</u> of
death was doubtful they might look to the other
facts—whereas he ought (I think it clear) to have said that
they were to look to all the evidence and facts bearing on the
cause of death and if in the result there was doubt—to acquit
even though the prisoner might have sought to poison her
husband.

Very strong feeling is very widely expressed and I hope you
will get the best reports of the evidence you can. I will send you
the local papers. (HO 144/1638/A50678)

Russell followed up with a seven-page memorandum to the
Home Office on 14 August (see plate 16). His covering letter

stated that 'the case demands independent examination by you'. The word 'independent' was underlined twice. What he meant was that Matthews should consider the case independently of Judge Stephen, whom he viewed as being part of the problem.

The conclusion of Russell's memorandum is worth quoting at some length:

> It is no exaggeration to say that every point made by the prosecution was put by the learned judge, and with greater insistence as well as other points which the prosecution had not made — while at the same time he does not seem to have realised the importance of many of the points made on the part of the prisoner, and did not put some of them at all and those which he did put he minimised and discounted.
>
> In short he had honestly if mistakenly taken the view that the woman was clearly guilty — that there was practically little to be said for her, and that view he persistently and vehemently impressed upon the jury in a summing up of two days and in a manner which would justify the trial being described as a trial by judge rather than jury.
>
> On the whole it is submitted that looking to all the facts — to the strange habits of the deceased, and to the strong conflict of the medical testimony — coupled with the summing up of the judge which took captive the judgment of the jury, the verdict cannot be regarded as satisfactory and the irrevocable penalty ought not to be inflicted.
>
> Lastly. It is important to note that the verdict came as a surprise upon the trained minds of the Bar of the Northern Circuit and that to the very last moment (even after the

summing up) the leading Counsel for the Prosecution Mr Addison Q.C., M.P. persisted in saying that the Jury could not (especially in view of the Medical evidence) find a verdict of guilty. (HO 144/1638/A50678)

Press clippings in the Home Office files dated 15 August 1889 show that the government was paying attention to the matter. An article titled 'Today's Chat' from an unidentified paper laid out the problem:

> If Mrs Maybrick gets a reprieve, as is most probable, the Judge will be inferentially censured. If not reprieved the Home Office will contract almost unprecedented unpopularity, dashed with execration. It will be said that the Home Secretary was swayed by interested advice, and that the woman was hanged to save the credit of the judge. This being so, it would, in my opinion, be best for the Home Office to act on its own unbiased judgment, without as is generally done in such cases consulting the judge. (HO 144/1638/A50678)

Another clipping, again from an unidentified newspaper, put the argument for a proper Court of Appeal, describing the process of appeal to the Home Office as 'secret and anti-British in its method of enquiry, capricious in operation, and unsatisfactory in its results' (HO 144/1638/A50678).

The press reaction reflected the level of public disquiet. All over the country discussions were taking place about Florence's innocence or guilt. Petitions poured into the Home Office; three were even dumped in the Home Secretary's lap as he sat on the

Treasury Bench in the House of Commons, an unprecedented
event. The Cleavers had a petition template printed in the newspapers for public use. Quantities of flowers and letters arrived
at Walton gaol for Florence. Seven men proposed to her. One
even offered to be hanged in her place, on the basis that if an
innocent person was to be executed, it might as well be he.
Madame Tussaud's was quick to jump on the bandwagon: its
waxwork of Florence at the entrance of the Napoleon room
attracted 50,000 visitors in two weeks.

The letters pages in the papers at this time give a vivid
picture of the public strength of feeling about the case. In the
Home Office files there is a scrapbook titled 'Mrs Maybrick's
Trial—Letters Favourable to a Reprieve' (HO 144/1638/A50678).
These letters were cut from the *Liverpool Daily Post*; clearly
the Home Office was paying attention to public opinion. One,
from the newspaper on 9 August 1889, is headed: 'He that is
without sin among you, let him cast a stone at her':

> Sir—The harshest judgments passed by women upon their
> more erring sisters are often reproved by men. Yet I doubt
> whether a jury of her own sex would have condemned Mrs
> Maybrick. If our law had allowed such a verdict they might
> have returned one of 'not proven' but surely any 12 intelligent
> English women would have felt it impossible to send to her
> death one of whose guilt there is grave doubt. They dare not
> have incurred the fearful responsibility of hurrying out of life
> the woman against whom that very responsibility has not been

proved, and they would I think have hesitated to brand with so deep a mark the innocent children who can never outgrow the injury of this harsh verdict. To a woman that verdict is simply inexplicable

Yours, Feminae

Someone calling himself 'Turned Around' even wrote to the *Liverpool Daily Post* on 15 August reporting a conversation he'd had with his gardener:

Sir — My gardener who is a quaint old Cheshire man of shrewd common sense has taken greatly to the Maybrick case… He goes on to say that his gardener said, 'So far as I can see Mr Maybrick took arsenic for his stummak [sic] or summat [sic] else and his wife took it on her face; that's evidence isn't it?' 'Yes,' I replied. 'Then who gave the fatal dose him or her? That's the doubt and in my opinion a big doubt…' I was confounded as I had always held she was guilty. That she is not convicted on legal evidence is clearer day by day.

Petitions flooded in from the legal and medical professions and from members of the public. Some protestors wrote directly to the Queen and the Prince and Princess of Wales. One petition in the Home Office records gives 30,000 names from the people of Manchester, including 449 merchants, 114 solicitors, 217 manufacturers, 14 physicians and surgeons, 6 barristers, 35 clergymen, 12 magistrates, 34 journalists and 10 bankers (HO 144/1638/A50678). Mass meetings were organized: one in London was led by a Scottish barrister, Alexander MacDougall, who campaigned for many years on Florence's behalf (see plate 19).

The jury that heard the Maybrick case came in for particular criticism. It was reported that during the trial jury members had been seen playing billiards in a hotel nearby and mingling with the public. They had also received all the newspapers every day—so how could they have remained unbiased?

There were of course those who thought the right result had been reached in any case. The *Lancet* concluded that in its 'unbiased opinion … the verdict arrived at was warranted by the evidence', while the *Liverpool Courier* argued that 'The monstrous assumption that the judge acted as a partisan bigot and that the jury were twelve men in whom ignorance and inhumanity reigned supreme was bound to be discarded as untenable and is already being repudiated' (quoted in Christie).

Opinion was also split on the other side of the Atlantic. Ryan quotes some entertaining pieces from the American papers. The *New York Times* went in for a no-holds-barred assault on Judge Stephen and the English in general:

> The character of this judge, as, indeed of all English judges has been almost incredibly hardened by the influence of this autocratic power. As a class they are the most conceited, dogmatic, body of men probably existing in the whole English-speaking world. From habitual dealing with the whole criminal class as vermin, they come to regard jurymen as a sort of servile race. Out of this has grown a monstrous abuse of the institution known as the charge to the jury. Justice Stephen had the

effrontery to harangue this Liverpool jury of artisans and small shopkeepers through a speech which took two days to deliver...

Having attacked the judge, the paper later went on to hurl insults at the Lord Chancellor, Lord Halsbury, whom it described as 'a little chuckle-headed, porker-jowled man, who looks more like the custodian of the royal gin bottle than of a conscience'.

The *New York Sun* was among Florence's detractors. It took a moralistic stance: 'The truth is Mrs Maybrick has been a very bad woman. Letters that were not read at the trial show her to have carried on a number of intrigues with different men and that she was a depraved and conscienceless wanton' (quoted in Christie).

Meanwhile, the Cleavers, as well as organizing the petitions, were getting affidavits sworn to cover some of the criticisms raised in Judge Stephen's summing up of the case. The Cleavers themselves swore some, as did John Baillie Knight (clarifying the nature of his relationship with Florence) and the Baroness von Roques. In her affidavit dated 16 August 1889 the Baroness explained why she had not given evidence:

Mr Cleaver the solicitor for my daughter proposed to me that I should give evidence at her trial as to my knowledge of the use of arsenic as a cosmetic, and of its use by my daughter for that purpose but I appealed to him not to expose me to the pain of appearing in court on such an occasion to give evidence as to what I apparently wrongly thought a trivial and unimportant point unless I might be allowed to testify to my experience of my daughter's blameless life. (HO 144/1638/A50678)

This doesn't altogether ring true. Perhaps it is more likely that the Cleavers were worried about what sort of impression the grand, unconventional Baroness might make in court and how she would hold up under cross-examination, especially given the press coverage speculating about her racy private life.

On 16 August a conference was convened at the Home Office to discuss the case. Present were Home Secretary Henry Matthews, Lord Halsbury (the Lord Chancellor), Judge Stephen, Drs Stevenson and Tidy, a Mr Lushington and Dr Poore, who was the Prince of Wales's doctor. A report of this meeting is given in HO 144/1638/A50678.

Matthews had the unenviable task of trying to make sense of the medical evidence. At the beginning he said somewhat plaintively to the doctors, 'I want you to reconcile your differences if you can.' There was little chance of that, but Matthews was determined to get to grips with the details:

> Matthews: How many pieces of liver did you take to establish uniformity of distribution?
>> Dr Stevenson: I snipped a little piece off here and there.
>> Matthews: How many?
>> Dr Stevenson: I suppose at least a dozen pieces.

The doctors tended to be slippery and disputatious, sticking to the positions they had adopted in court. They even differed as to women's shopping habits:

> Matthews: Assuming that one dozen flypapers were purchased on 26th [this date was incorrect] for cosmetics can you explain

why two dozen more are required on the 29th?

Dr Stevenson: No.

Matthews: The two dozen flypapers disappeared from the case altogether.

Dr Stevenson: One flypaper would make a cosmetic at least.

Dr Tidy: Women do not stick at small quantities.

Judge Stephen's comments are intriguing. A suggestion by Dr Poore led to the following exchange:

Dr Poore: Is it conceivable that Mrs Maybrick gave him the arsenic herself in the Indian fashion as a love phille [sic], so to say; that he was not sexually not quite what he should be and she gave it to him with that notion?

Stephen: It seems to me almost impossible.

Matthews: No, no.

Stevenson: She expressed great repugnance to the man.

Matthews: They were quarrelling.

Stephen: One expression she used produced a great effect on my mind. She said she had a great repugnance to him. It was a kind of personal malice. According to one witness she said she hated her husband.

At the end of the conference Judge Stephen accurately summed up the situation when he said that 'you get a contradiction between two experts which you cannot reconcile'.

While Matthews was trying to reconcile the irreconcilable, Florence was being held in Walton gaol, guarded day and night by two female warders. This is how she described it in her book:

> Many have asked me what my feelings were at that awful time.
> I remember little in the way of details as to my state of mind. I
> was too overwhelmed for either analytic or collective thought...
> death seemed to me a blessed escape from a world in which
> such an unspeakable travesty of justice could take place...

Matthews came to his decision. Early on the morning of 23 August, three days before she was due to be hanged, Florence received momentous news. She wrote about how she was visited by the governor, the chaplain and a warder: 'The governor hastening forward exclaimed in an agitated voice: "It is well; it is good news!" When I opened my eyes once more I was lying in bed in the hospital.'

The commutation of Florence's sentence was announced to the press in the following way:

> We are given to understand that the Home Secretary, after
> fullest consideration and after taking the best legal and medical
> advice that could be obtained, has advised Her Majesty to
> respite the capital punishment of Florence Elizabeth Maybrick
> and to commute the punishment to penal servitude for life;
> inasmuch as, although the evidence leads to the conclusion that
> the prisoner administered and attempted to administer arsenic
> to her husband, with intent to murder him, yet it does not
> wholly exclude a reasonable doubt whether his death was in
> fact caused by the administration of arsenic. This decision is
> understood not to imply the slightest reflection on the able and
> experienced practitioners who gave evidence, or on the tribunal
> before which the prisoner was tried. We understand that the

course adopted has the concurrence of the learned judge.

(HO 144/1639/A50678)

Essentially Matthews had settled for a good, old-fashioned fudge. Public opinion being so strongly in favour of Florence Maybrick, he probably felt he could not let the sentence stand—but if he had released her he would have cast doubt on the whole judicial process. Instead he found Florence guilty of attempted murder and sentenced her to life imprisonment, which in those days was 20 years. But the fact was that she had never been tried for *attempted* murder. If she had been, the prosecution would have had to prove different facts and the defence would also have been different. At the time the decision spared the blushes of the judge and the establishment. Six years later, however, when the case was reviewed, a Home Office memo would describe 'the *damnosa hereditas* [damaging inheritance] of Mr Matthews's decision' (HO 144/1639/A50678). It was to haunt all Home Secretaries until Florence's release.

*The Times* expressed its opinion of Matthews's decision the following day: 'The case against Mrs Maybrick was and remains a case of terribly strong suspicion, but suspicion which after all is said just misses moral certainty... [the decision] makes things comfortable all round for the experts.'

After the initial euphoria died down Florence was now left facing 20 years in prison.

## CRUSADE FOR FREEDOM

Florence was removed to Woking prison and began a period of nine months' solitary confinement. This was followed by a second nine-month period of confinement called probation during which she was moved to a larger cell with a bed to sleep in rather than a hammock. After this she began hard labour in the prison kitchens. Meanwhile her numerous supporters on both sides of the Atlantic began working tirelessly in an effort to secure her release. They had to tread a fine line between grovelling to the establishment and expressing their outrage at the injustice to Florence.

Baroness von Roques was an indefatigable campaigner for her daughter, but one petition to the Queen on 23 May 1890 was unlikely to be well received: it was in illegible handwriting, peppered with exclamation marks and underlining, and included two pages of her family tree. The Baroness began: 'It is I fear presumptuous and almost unpardonable to express my opinion against that of your Majesty's responsible advisers…' Later on she stated: 'My second husband was the grandson of Benjamin Franklin … personally known and well thought of by the late Emperor Napoleon the third' (HO 144/1639/A50678).

Queen Victoria (see plate 17) was a woman known to worship at the shrine of her dead husband, Prince Albert. It was unlikely that she would take kindly to references to all of the Baroness's husbands, but given the appalling handwriting the petition was written in it is doubtful whether she even tried to read it.

In 1891 the Baroness moved to Rouen, although she came back every two months to see Florence and continued to hound the Home Office. It was in Rouen that a prescription for a face wash containing arsenic, written by a Dr Bay of New York, fell out of Florence's bible (see plate 20). The word 'Brouant' was stamped on it: this was the name of a Parisian chemist who had supplied the prescription back in 1878. The Baroness showed it to Alexander MacDougall, who contacted Brouant in Paris and, having received a certified copy of the entry from his records (HO 144/1640/A50678), got the Baroness and her maid to swear affidavits. This evidence was filed away for future use in the event of a retrial.

On 7 August 1891 the Americans became more actively involved. Helen Densmore, an American doctor, had been pivotal in setting up the Women's International Maybrick Association. One of her contacts, the author Miss Mary Dodge (her pen name was Gail Hamilton), was the cousin of Mrs Blaine, wife of the Secretary of State. As a result of these contacts a petition to the Queen of England was signed by the wives of the President, the Secretary of State, the Secretary of the Treasury and the Secretary of Agriculture. It said:

> The four and fifty years of your illustrious reign have established you in the respect and love of the citizens of this Republic. Confiding in the power of your Majesty and in the power of your goodness we pray your grace on behalf of our

young countrywoman, Florence Maybrick, a widow, a mother, fatherless, brotherless, wearing out in prison...

(HO 144/1639/A50678)

Back from Balmoral, on 2 October 1891, came a note with a thick black mourning border stating: 'The Queen entirely approves and agrees with Mr Matthews on the case of Mrs Maybrick' (see plate 18; HO 144/1639/A50678).

The following year, on 1 June, another even more heavy-weight petition arrived at the Home Office, this time signed by the Vice-President of the United States, Levi P. Morton; the speaker of the House of Representatives; an enormous number of brigadier-generals; the General in Chief of the army of the United States; Cardinal Gibbons, the head of the Catholic Church in the USA; the Paymaster General and four assistant paymaster generals. It sent the Home Office into a rage.

A civil servant wrote in red ink across the Home Office file 'This petition bears most influential names'. Another one wrote revealing the Home Office view: 'A truly astonishing document: for if ever there was a criminal not entitled to mercy it is Mrs Maybrick. How persons occupying stations of such high re-sponsibility could sign this document on a slight and imperfect knowledge of the facts I cannot imagine' (HO 144/1639/A50678).

The Home Office had made up its mind and was to stick rigidly to this point of view. The petition was turned down.

In 1892 the Liberals came to power and in September of that year the new Home Secretary, Herbert Asquith, announced that no further action would be taken on the case.

Maybe because of this, and the rejection of the American petitions, Florence despaired and decided to take matters into her own hands. In November 1892 she petitioned the Home Office for her release on the grounds of ill health. On the same day the prison doctor also wrote stating that:

> her health has recently shown a tendency to deteriorate. She daily shows a quantity of blood which she alleges she has spit up but I am not able by physical examination to find any evidence to corroborate her statement and am inclined to believe the blood spitting to be fictitious... (HO 144/1639/A50678)

Confined in the hospital ward, Florence was spied on by the matron. Dr Glover, the Medical Inspector of Woking prison, reported to the Home Office:

> She stealthily placed the spitting cup in the chamber on the floor, then reached down for her dinner knife from the shelf, introduced the knife as far as the matron could see, into the vagina and withdrew it covered with blood. She then appeared to kneel over the chamber. The woman's object was no doubt to incise the mucous membrane of the vagina just so far as to give rise to slight bleeding, and then to catch the blood in the spittoon placed in the chamber. (HO 144/1639/A50678)

Florence's attempt to prove she had tuberculosis came close to killing her. When she did the same thing the following day she divided the vaginal artery, haemorrhaged and almost died.

The Baroness hammered away at the Home Office: could

she see her daughter fortnightly because she was so ill and for longer than the 20 minutes that was strictly allowed? In the same letter she asks that she might send 'a little photograph of myself', for Florence to keep in her cell. All these requests were met with a censorious response from the Home Office. A civil servant wrote on one file during this time that: 'she [Florence] knows by this time that her malingering has been discovered'. And the Baroness's request for fortnightly visits was turned down on the basis that 'it would make her [Florence] more difficult to manage and influence' (HO 144/1639/A50698).

Sir Charles Russell was equally indefatigable in Florence's support. On 27 June 1895, now Lord Chief Justice and Lord Russell of Killowen, he wrote to Florence:

> I beg to assure you that I have never relaxed my efforts where
> any suitable opportunity offered to urge that your release
> ought to be granted. I feel as strongly as I have felt from the
> first that you ought never to have been convicted, and this
> opinion I have very clearly expressed to Mr Asquith, but I am
> sorry to say hitherto without effect.

Five years later, when this letter was forwarded to the Home Office by Florence's current solicitor Mr Clark Bell, a civil servant wrote that 'This letter does not express any opinion as to convicts innocence. It merely expresses the opinion she ought not to have been convicted. Nothing new here' (HO 144/1640/A50678).

Russell was true to his word. He took the opportunity of another change of government to send off a ferocious letter to

Sir Matthew White-Ridley, the new Home Secretary, on 21 November 1895. In it he states that 'Florence Maybrick ought never to have been convicted, and that, her continued imprisonment is an injustice which ought promptly to be ended. I have never wavered in this opinion' (HO 144/1640/A50678).

Judge Stephen was now dead. After questions had been raised in the Commons about his competence he had been forced to resign in April 1891, and in 1894 he died in an insane asylum in Ipswich. Russell could therefore be much freer with his criticisms and stated in his letter of 21 November that 'I never thought Mr Justice Stephen a good judge'. He continued: 'I feel absolutely convinced that had not his powers been at the time of this trial distinctly on the wane, this miscarriage of justice could not have occurred... the foundation on which the whole case rested was rotten: for that in fact there was no murder.' He went on to make some interesting comments:

an error of judgment was made in trying the case at Liverpool... the Maybricks were a Liverpool family... the crime charged was an atrocious crime and the Brierley episode had alienated the sympathies of many and predisposed to a conclusion of guilt. Lastly on this head the newspapers had indulged in more than the usual license of comment and the public was saturated with prejudice.

He finished by throwing down a challenge:

I know that it requires some strength of judgment to order the release of Florence Maybrick, when Mr Matthews and Mr

Asquith have not done so. It is the resource of weak men to
shelter themselves behind the action or inaction of others. I do
not for an instant harbour the idea that you are one of those men.

Unfortunately for Florence, White-Ridley was just such a man.
Russell's letter was forwarded by the Home Office to Lord
Halsbury, the Lord Chancellor, who had been involved in the
original decision, and back came the reply that 'the convict was
guilty and the action taken by Secretary Matthews was right'
(HO 144/1640/A50678). Halsbury was hardly likely to recommend
anything else.

On 20 February 1896 Russell received the following feeble
reply from the Home Secretary: 'I can only express my regret
that a sense of my public duty prevents me recommending any
further extension of the clemency of the crown' (HO 144/1640A50678).
And when the House of Commons requested that Russell's
opinion be made accessible to its members, White-Ridley refused,
presumably on the grounds that it would increase agitation for
Florence's release and make more trouble for himself.

In refusing to consider all the petitions on Florence's behalf
it may have been that the Home Office felt that its hands were
tied by the attitude of Queen Victoria. *The Letters of Queen
Victoria*, edited by George Earle Buckle, includes the following
communication from the Queen to Matthews at the time of the
commutation of Mrs Maybrick's sentence: 'The only regret she
feels about the decision is that so wicked a woman should escape
by a mere legal quibble! The law is not a moral profession she

must say. But her sentence must never be further commuted.'

This was certainly the conclusion that the American government eventually reached. Christie cites the following memorandum, written in 1897, from Under-Secretary of State Alvey Adee to the new Secretary of State, John Sherman:

> It is understood that the Queen is inflexibly convinced of Mrs Maybrick's guilt and will permit no appeal on her behalf. The successive Home Secretaries who have refused to reopen the case are understood to have acted under the Queen's peremptory orders. A direct request to the crown is useless ... there is not the slightest chance of Mrs Maybrick being released during the Queen's lifetime.

Queen Victoria, a woman who thought that women's rights were 'mad, wicked folly' and that suffragettes deserved a 'good whipping', a woman who had adored her own husband, seems to have believed that Florence had tried to poison her husband and was an evil and immoral woman who deserved to be in prison. No Home Secretary was going to change her mind.

There was something else that may have made the Home Office feel that it had made the right decision. On 10 February 1890 the Head Constable of Liverpool, William Nott-Bower, wrote to the Home Secretary:

> I have the honour to inform you that I have heard on what I believe to be reliable authority that evidence can be obtained as to where Mrs Maybrick procured arsenic.
>
> My informant (who is connected to the press) declines to

divulge names, but states that the chemist who supplied the
arsenic is willing to come forward and make a full statement.

(HO 144/1639/A50678)

It is unclear exactly what the Home Office did about this at the
time. The letter may just have confirmed what they already
believed: that Florence Maybrick was guilty.

But in 1926 the letter emerged in public for the first time on
the publication of Sir William Nott-Bower's memoirs, *Fifty-
Two Years a Policeman*. A press cutting from the *Weekly
Despatch* dated 17 January 1926 quotes from Nott-Bower's
book and gives more details:

> He [the chemist, Richard Aspinall of 1 Leece Street] said that
> in the spring of 1889 Mrs Maybrick drove up to his shop in her
> dogcart and asked for powdered arsenic to kill rats (or cats), and
> he supplied her with a large quantity, which she took away with her.
>
> A week or two later she again drove up to his shop and told
> him she had lost the arsenic she had from him and asked for
> more which he supplied her. (HO 144/1639/A50678)

Aspinall had not come forward because he was worried about
being prosecuted under the Sale of Drugs and Poisons Act,
which specified that chemists should keep detailed records of
who they sold poison to. The fact that the sale was not on the
record—apparently at Florence's request—was damning for
her, as was the quantity of arsenic and the fact that no one at
the trial could come up with an innocent explanation for its
presence in Battlecrease House.

However, another explanation for the presence of that packet was provided by a man named Valentine Blake. This emerged after Jonathan Harris, a London solicitor now employed by the Baroness, put out a newspaper advert in 1893 asking for anyone with evidence relating to the Maybrick case to come forward. Blake swore an affidavit stating that he had written to the Cleavers at the time of the trial but had received no reply. At the time his son was lost at sea and he was overcome with grief, so he had not pursued the matter. He said that he had come across James Maybrick in January 1889 when he was trying to launch a new cloth product called ramie on to the market. Arsenic was involved in its manufacture. After relating a conversation between the pair about Thomas de Quincey's *Confessions of an English Opium Eater*, Blake's affidavit continues:

> The said James Maybrick said, 'One man's poison is another man's meat and there is a so-called poison which is like meat and liquor to me whenever I feel weak and depressed; it makes me stronger in mind and in body at once' or words to that effect. I ventured to ask him what it was. He answered 'I don't tell everybody and wouldn't tell you only you mentioned arsenic. It is Arsenic. I take it when I can get it but the doctors won't put any into my medication except now and then a trifle that only tantalizes me.' (HO 144/1639/A50678)

When James asked him for some arsenic, Blake replied that 'I had no license to sell drugs and suggested we should make it a quid pro quo. Mr Maybrick was to do his best with the ramie grass product and I was to make him a present of the arsenic I had.' In other words, a bribe.

Blake continued: 'I handed him all the arsenic I had at my command, amounting to 150 grains, some of the "white" and some of the two kinds of "black" arsenic in three separate packets... I told him to be careful as he had almost enough to poison a regiment.'

The contents of the affidavit were confirmed by Blake's employer. This would explain why the arsenic found at Battlecrease House was not mixed with soot or indigo but charcoal. Its original use was for industrial purposes, not public purchase.

Harris also managed to unearth Nurse Yapp, now Mrs Marrer, whose husband wrote to the Home Office in January 1894 to complain that his wife was being harassed by Harris's private detective. The detective had apparently said to Yapp, 'Of course people blame you very much. Mrs Briggs and yourself have cooked it up' (HO 144/1639/A50698). Mr Marrer went on to say that he would have to leave his present address because his wife was 'continually weeping and thoroughly depressed'.

In the spring of 1896 Florence was transferred from Woking to Aylesbury where the regime was not so strict, but despite this she suffered a nervous breakdown. In August of that year the Baroness petitioned the Home Office for her daughter's release on the basis that she was in a 'dying condition'. In a letter to the American Secretary of State, Olney, on 29 September 1896, she described her daughter as 'weak, emaciated, grey in colour, like a dead person ... her voice is a whisper and her attitude despair, frequent fainting fits occur' (HO 144/1640/A50678).

The Home Office was worried enough to seek a report from the prison authorities. Back it came:

> we have failed to discover any evidence of any organic disease... In spite of this she has, during the past four months, exhibited symptoms of great nervous depression... I have urged her to try and rouse herself but she says she has nothing to live for, that she has lost all hope, and that her only wish is that she may die speedily. (HO 144/1640/A50678)

One cause of Florence's depression may have been that in 1895 Michael Maybrick, now her children's guardian, had stopped sending her the annual photos of her children. When she asked about this she was told that it was because her son, James, didn't want her to receive them any more.

The following year was the Queen's diamond jubilee and there were high hopes that Florence might be pardoned. A telegram was sent to the American Embassy: 'the President suggests that, if brought to the attention of her Majesty she might welcome the present as a most fitting opportunity to extend mercy' (HO 144/1640/A50678). But the Queen was not inclined to extend mercy: again the Home Office turned the request down.

Early in 1900 Sir Charles Russell visited Florence in her cell and they spoke for half an hour. In her book Florence recounts that he told her, 'Be brave be strong, I believe you to be an innocent woman. I have done and will continue to do all I can for you.'

Russell wrote to the Home Secretary again, but a few months later he died after a short illness. In the end all his efforts on behalf of the woman he had termed the 'friendless lady' had, like those of the Baroness, the Women's International Maybrick Association, Alexander MacDougall and the American government, come to nothing. The Home Office had refused to budge an inch.

On 22 January 1901, however, Queen Victoria herself died, and within six months the Home Office was considering its options. A Home Office memo to Mr Ritchie, the Home Secretary, on 10 July 1901 states that:

> It would be possible to fix 15 years as the period at which she might be brought up for licence. I think it would be well, if this decision is come to, to inform the American Ambassador at the interview on Friday that it has been so decided and to communicate the decision to the prisoner. This will give her 3 more years to serve. I think it should be understood that although in the ordinary course she will be licensed when she has served 15 years that decision is not irrevocable but will depend on her conduct, and that the difficulty of acting on it will be increased if agitation against the justice of her conviction is renewed.
> (HO 144/1640/A50678)

Florence's conduct must have been satisfactory, for after all those long years in prison she was released on 20 January 1904. She had become friendly with the Duchess of Bedford, a prison visitor, during her time at Aylesbury, and the Duchess arranged for her to spend her six months' probation in a convent at Truro. On the morning of 20 January 1904 Florence set aside her horrible prison garb and dressed in a smart new outfit her mother had sent from Paris. In the company of Miss Stewart, the principal matron, she left Aylesbury prison and travelled to London. There the noise and bustle of the capital frightened her and she clung to her escort's arm. From Paddington station they took the train to Truro. In her autobiography Florence described her time there as 'the most peaceful and the happiest—in the true sense—of my whole life'.

When the six months had passed Florence travelled to France on 20 July 1904 to be reunited with her mother, and then made the trip back across the Atlantic to America. It was a highly emotional journey for her. She wrote: 'When I first caught sight of the Statue of Liberty, I, perhaps more than anyone on board, realized the full meaning of what it typifies, and I felt my heart stirred to its depths…' As she set foot on the gangplank to disembark, the ship's band struck up 'Home, Sweet Home' and she burst into tears.

Thousands of people were there to greet Mrs Maybrick. As she climbed into the Densmores' waiting carriage, a little girl threw a bouquet of flowers to her.

# CHAPTER FIVE

# The Past is Dead

While Florence stayed with the Densmores on arrival in America, she wrote the flowery and self-dramatizing *My Fifteen Lost Years*. She then signed up to the Slayton Lyceum Bureau of Chicago and began a series of lectures on prison reform. A freak attraction, she was to make between 75 and 100 lectures at an average fee of $50 each. Florence needed the money: she and her mother were practically penniless and unable to rely on the generosity of friends for ever. Her manager Charles Wagner in his book *Seeing Stars* (1940) described her like this:

> Her face was the stillest I have ever gazed upon. It was as isolated from the real meaning of life as a white sheet of paper before it receives the printed impression. It had no cry, no need, no desire, no hunger, but it looked just to me. It stood for what fifteen years of life in an English prison can do to sterilize a human countenance. (quoted in Christie)

By 1910 Florence had fetched up in the Moraine Hotel, Illinois, which was owned by Frederick Cushing. Interest in her was waning, and although she was only 48 years old her health was failing; she was unable to continue with her lectures or pay her bill. On enquiring what her plans were, Cushing was told by Florence that she had no money but did have an interest in two million acres in the South. For the next couple of years he pursued her case and allowed her to stay at the hotel at his expense.

During this period two deaths occurred. The Baroness died in a French convent, while Florence's son, James, who had been working as a mining engineer in Canada, was killed in a bizarre accident in which he was said to have mistakenly drunk hydrochloric acid. When informed of his death Florence said, according to the *Chicago Daily Tribune* of 10 May 1911: 'I have no son. The past is dead. The boy has been dead to me for more than twenty years' (quoted in Graham and Emmas).

There was more bad news. Cushing informed her that she would get nothing from her properties. When he offered to help set her up in an old people's home, she said she 'would prefer to starve in a gutter'. Instead, she worked for the publisher Shuman and Company selling books door to door, but when her health failed again she pawned her belongings, became a vagrant and was looked after by the Salvation Army in Chicago.

She next appears in the winter of 1917 in Kent, Connecticut, calling herself Florence Chandler. While in New York Florence had become friends with a woman named Cora Griffin, who found her a job as housekeeper to Henrietta Banwell, a Kent chicken farmer. Housekeeping, however, had never been Florence's strong point. She and the Banwells parted company, but she stayed in the area. Her finances had obviously recovered because she bought a plot of land on which she built herself a house. Here she remained for the rest of her life. The house had no running water, but there were three rooms, a pot-bellied stove and a six-foot porch giving beautiful views of the Housatonic Valley.

Florence was receiving money at this time from Alden Freeman, a philanthropist who had arranged for her to give one of her lectures in New Jersey. After her death it was discovered that 12 different people had been giving her money during this period, none of them aware of the others. Cora Griffin was another of those benefactors, although she eventually stopped because she thought Florence spent too much money on her cats. Christie quotes interesting descriptions given of Florence by three women who knew her at this period. Griffin's opinion was that: 'She thought the world owed her a living. She leaned on strangers too much, and she took their help for granted.' Griffin is also reported to have said that Florence was 'a little mentally unbalanced', but that she had a 'will of steel'.

Relying on the charity of others proved trickier during the 1930s when the depression hit America. Florence had become friends with Clara Dulon, a matron at the local boys' school, who found work for her with Mrs Robertson, the wife of the school chaplain. Mrs Robertson gave a more generous description of Florence:

> I encouraged her to linger with me many times when her work was done and I enjoyed her. She seemed to me a very unusual

personality, the finest example I had almost ever seen of
buoyant courage in the utmost adversity. I soon discovered she
was telling me some incredible things to dramatise herself, but
this seemed to me a natural and excusable psychological devel-
opment for one in her situation as I understood it.

After Dulon died Florence would come and visit the school
nurse, Amy Lyon, who reported that:

They [the boys at the school] thought her very interesting and
often asked who she was, living alone in her little shack in the
woods. They thought she was a lady... she often cried and tears
rolled down her cheeks. I sat down beside her and asked her
why she cried. She would say it makes me feel better.

As the years passed old age began to catch up with Florence,
her eccentricity predictably evolving into something altogether
sadder. She struggled to keep herself clean, wrapping herself
in blankets which she held together with pins and wearing a
woolly hat irrespective of the weather. She walked every day to
the local shop for a newspaper and set up feeding stations for
stray cats and dogs. If a car stopped to offer her a lift she would
hide in the bushes or claim that her legs were too stiff for her to
get in. Her house became derelict and filthy; her colony of cats
expanded; her flowerbeds grew neglected.

In October 1941 Florence suffered a mild stroke. She
refused to be taken to hospital and died two days later. Among
her effects were a recipe explaining how to cure cats of gastritis,
an address book with the 'G's torn out, several photos including

one of her children, bits of jewellery, two rosaries and the family bible that had held the face wash prescription. She left her property to the South Kent School, and boys from the school carried her coffin to the grave where she was buried next to her friend, Clara Dulon. The wooden cross stated: 'F.E.C.M. 1862–1941'. While her coffin was being lowered into the earth locals were surprised to see the police holding a crowd of reporters at bay. The press knew that the famous Florence Maybrick had died. Her secret was out, but could no longer harm her.

Mrs Maybrick may have died alone in a filthy hovel with only cats for company but she had at least died on her own terms, not in an old people's home or a hospital. Whatever else one thinks about Florence, one thing is indisputable: she was a survivor. She died at the age of 79, which, when one considers what she had gone through in her life, showed an iron will indeed.

## 'HORRIBLE WOMAN' OR 'FRIENDLESS LADY'?

Why does the Maybrick case continue to fascinate? Perhaps partly because, even though it took place over a hundred years ago, some aspects of it are very recognizable today. What did Florence do when her affair fell through? She went shopping for handbags. What did Madam Tussaud's do when she was found guilty? Made a waxwork of her. How did the press behave? Well, very like the 'feral beasts' so decried by Tony Blair. And what of the sexual double standard? It would be a naïve person who claimed that sexual double standards don't still exist. Present-day victims of rape might well argue that the criminal justice system has quite a way to go before we can claim to be much more enlightened than our Victorian ancestors.

Another reason for the fascination may be that there are sufficient gaps and oddities in the Maybrick case to allow theories about what really happened to flourish. For example, in *The Last Victim* Graham and Emmas put the case that James Maybrick was in fact Jack the Ripper, and that it wasn't Florence who killed her husband but Michael Maybrick, who discovered James's crimes and wanted to protect the family name.

Although this particular theory (based on a forged diary) seems to lack credibility, it is impossible to read about the Maybrick case without indulging in a little speculation as to whether Florence killed her husband or not. There's no doubt that she should not have been convicted on the evidence—but of course that is not the same as saying that she was innocent.

Here, briefly, are the two sides of the argument.

## THE CASE FOR FLORENCE'S GUILT

Florence Maybrick, arguably, was as Judge Stephen said 'a horrible woman': a cunning, conniving murderess. She was tired of her elderly, philandering, maybe impotent, drug addict husband and wanted to be rid of him and free to marry her younger lover, Alfred Brierley. She discussed James's drug taking with Michael Maybrick and two doctors in order to set up a defence for herself, aware that her husband's inveterate drug use meant that it would be extremely difficult to prove she had killed him. Embarking on an affair with Brierley, she panicked when found out. She argued with her husband at the Grand National and he hit her afterwards. This was the last straw. There was no reconciliation, and she decided to poison him.

Florence knew that flypapers contained arsenic because of the famous Flanagan and Higgins case of 1884: she bought two sets of flypapers in quick succession because she was using up the arsenic liquid in poisoning her husband. At first she used Du Barry's invalid food to convey the arsenic, but she was an incompetent poisoner, not using large enough quantities to succeed—or James wasn't eating enough of the food. But on Friday 4 May James Maybrick ate all the food he had taken to the office in a jug: the fatal dose. He hurried home and died a week later. Arsenic was found on the lip of the jug.

She was still trying to poison James while he was bedridden, this time using Valentine's meat juice, and so arsenic was found in the Valentine's bottle and on her clothes and handkerchief. Enough poison was found in the house 'to kill a regiment'. Maybe she also bought the packet marked 'Poison for Cats' and persuaded the chemist not to write down her name on the register. When her husband finally died she could not cope with her conscience and collapsed in a hysterical swoon—or was aware of the suspicions against her and so couldn't risk running around the house disposing of all the poisons, which were then found unhidden. At any rate, having made sure that enough people knew about James's drug taking, she knew that she could blame the presence of the drugs in Battlecrease House, and James Maybrick's death, on this habit, and that this would cast doubt on her guilt.

Florence Maybrick was guilty, and when her sentence was commuted she got away with murder. She then played the role of innocent victim for the rest of her life, expertly manipulating the pity this generated to extract money from people.

## THE CASE FOR FLORENCE'S INNOCENCE

On the other hand, perhaps Florence Maybrick was an innocent but rather naïve woman. She was worried about her husband's drug taking and did not like the effect it had on him, which was why she discussed it with Michael and the doctors. She had an affair with Brierley but was reconciled with her husband after the quarrel at the Grand National. While he was in London paying off her debts she wrote him a remorseful letter which demonstrates this. She bought the flypapers to use as a facial cosmetic because she wanted to get rid of an outbreak of spots before she went to a ball with Edwin Maybrick. She had had a prescription for a face wash made up for her before, which contained arsenic, but had lost it; it came to light after her trial.

James Maybrick's system had been undermined by his

chronic drug consumption. Having taken a double dose of Dr
Fuller's medicine on 26 April 1889, he foolishly went out riding
and got soaked. He himself said in his letter to his brother that
he thought Dr Fuller had poisoned him. Further weakened by a
day spent at the Wirral races, he developed gastro-enteritis.
The arsenic found in his body was put there by himself, while
that found on the lip of the jug used at his office was present
because he had put arsenic in his own food. That found in the
Valentine's meat juice was placed there by Florence at his
request, as reported in her court statement. When she spilled
this she got it on her handkerchief, dressing gown and apron.

Florence Maybrick nursed her husband attentively, called in
another doctor, Dr Carter, when she was worried about his
condition and asked for nursing help when she could no longer
cope. When he died she collapsed with exhaustion and grief.
The presence of all the drugs and poisons can be explained by
James's extreme hypochondria and drug habit. The explanation of the packet of arsenic lies in the evidence supplied by
Valentine Blake after the trial. In her statement Florence
admitted putting the powder in the bottle of Valentine's meat
juice. She would never have done this if she was guilty.

## A PERSONAL VIEW

It is chastening to consider that if Mrs Maybrick was innocent,
she was the victim of backbiting servants, malicious so-called

friends and vindictive in-laws. Friendless indeed, just as Russell had said. Her husband died, her children were removed and she was abandoned and held under house arrest. She was forbidden to go to her own husband's funeral. She was thrown into prison. Her brothers-in-law sold off the contents of her house against the wishes of her husband as stated in his will. She had the misfortune to come up against a judge whose mental health was failing. Through a terrible miscarriage of justice she was found guilty of a crime she had not committed.

Then, because the establishment didn't know how to deal with a mentally impaired judge, she was sacrificed by the government so that society's faith in the criminal justice system should not be undermined. She served 15 years for a crime —attempted murder—she had not been tried for, and never saw her children again. All efforts to free her were blocked by the Queen, who deeply disapproved of her marital infidelity and thought her guilty of murder—and by a Home Office that refused to admit that the decision reached by Henry Matthews in 1889 was a bad one. Her health was destroyed and her life ruined by the incompetence of the judge and the establishment's determination to protect his and its own reputation.

I don't think Florence Maybrick did it. She comes across as someone more impulsive than calculating, and poisoners are never impulsive. She had shown herself incapable of keeping her affair secret, so what would have made her think she would get away with murder? She was not trapped in the marriage because she had the grounds to divorce James if she wanted to be rid of him. So why take the risk of poisoning him? Her background was—to put it mildly—unconventional for the times; divorce in itself would not have horrified her. She was undoubtedly fey, frivolous, rather snobbish and prone to self-dramatizing; it's easy to imagine that she irritated people. Rather than a cunning murderess it seems likely that she was indeed a naïve woman, who did a number of silly things in fatal sequence and thus aroused suspicion—the affair, buying the flypapers, writing the letter to Brierley, putting the powder in the bottle of Valentine's meat juice at her husband's request. But she ended up paying for this foolishness with 15 years of her life. After that, no wonder she thought the world owed her a living, no wonder she thought the company of inbred cats an altogether safer proposition than that of humans.

This is how Florence ended her book:

> A time will come when the world will acknowledge that the verdict which was passed upon me is absolutely untenable. But what then? Who will give me back the years I have spent within prison walls; the friends by whom I am forgotten; the children to whom I am dead; the sunshine; the winds of heaven; my woman's life, and all I have lost by this terrible injustice?

Was Florence Judge Stephen's 'horrible woman' or Russell's 'friendless lady'? You choose.

# Sources & Reading

The National Archives has extensive Home Office files relating to
Florence Maybrick in HO 144/1638/A50678–HO 144/1641/A50678.
These include an original letter from Florence and a facsimile of her
famous letter to Brierley intercepted by Nurse Yapp, a complete
report of the trial in the *Liverpool Daily Post* and depositions for the
coroner's inquest and magistrates' hearing. There is also a full record
of the meeting on 16 August 1889 between the Home Secretary,
Judge Stephen and the two doctors who took opposing views, as
well as Home Office correspondence with the American government,
Baroness von Roques and the prison authorities. The Archives also
holds copyrighted photographs of Florence Maybrick registered in
the year of her trial (COPY 1 396–8). See www.nationalarchives.gov.uk for
the catalogue and visiting information.

The best book to start with is Trevor Christie's *Etched in Arsenic*
which, although out of print, is worth tracking down. It is immensely
readable and entertaining and the first book to pull together all
the different strands of the story. If that cannot be found, then *The
Poisoned Life of Mrs Maybrick* by Bernard Ryan is a good starting
point. The theory that James Maybrick was really Jack the Ripper is
expounded in *The Last Victim* by Anne E. Graham and Carol Emmas,
while *Elements of Murder* by John Emsley is an account that finds
Florence guilty. *The Trial of Mrs Maybrick*, edited by H.B. Irving,
gives a transcript of the court proceedings. Florence Maybrick's own

book is disappointing and mainly useful as an account of the regime in women's prisons in Victorian England.

G.E. Buckle (ed.), *The Letters of Queen Victoria*, vol. 1 (John Murray, 1930)

T. Christie, *Etched in Arsenic* (Harrap, 1968)

M. Diamond, *Victorian Sensation* (Anthem Press, 2004)

J. Emsley, *The Elements of Murder: A History of Poison* (Oxford University Press, 2005)

A.E. Graham and C. Emmas, *The Last Victim* (Headline, 1999)

W.T. Harries, *Landmarks in Liverpool History* (Philip Son & Nephew, 1946)

H.B. Irving (ed.), *The Trial of Mrs Maybrick* (Notable British Trials series, William Hodge & Co., 1927)

A.W. MacDougall, *The Maybrick Case: A Treatise* (Bailliere, Tindall & Cox, 1891)

F. Maybrick, *Mrs Maybrick's Own Story: My Fifteen Lost Years* (Funk & Wagnalls, 1909)

R. O'Brien, *Life of Lord Russell of Killowen* (Smith, Elder & Co., 1901)

B. Ryan, *The Poisoned Life of Mrs Maybrick* (Penguin, 1989)

L. Stephen, *Life of Sir James Fitzjames Stephen* (Smith, Elder & Co., 1895)

## ACKNOWLEDGEMENTS

The Author would like to thank Catherine Bradley, Gillian Hawkins and Sheila Knight at the National Archives for their enthusiasm and professionalism, also Steve Gove for his meticulous eye for detail.

Pictures can be seen at the National Archives unless another source is given here.
**1** Topfoto/UPPA/Photoshot **3** © TopFoto; TopFoto.co.uk **6**, **7**, **15** Getty Images
**12** Mary Evans Picture Library **13** Time & Life Pictures/Getty Images

# Index